MY MOTHER ALWAYS SAYS

MY MOTHER ALWAYS SAYS

25 Lessons for Finding the Silver Lining

AMY GOOBER AND **GWEN BORDEN**

DRIVE YOUR LIFE PUBLISHING

Copyright © 2025 by Amy Goober

All rights reserved.

No part of this book may be reproduced, or stored in a retrieval system, or transmitted in any form or by any means, electronic, mechanical, photocopying, recording, or otherwise, without express written permission of the publisher.

Published by Drive Your Life Publishing, Woburn, MA
https://amygoober.com

Edited and designed by Girl Friday Productions
www.girlfridayproductions.com

Cover design: Megan Katsanevakis

ISBN (hardcover): 979-8-9922684-0-9
ISBN (ebook): 979-8-9922684-1-6

Library of Congress Control Number: 2025902368

First edition

CONTENTS

Intro vii
1. How Lucky Can You Be? 1
2. Alone in the Dark 10
3. More Than Just a Degree 24
4. Flying Solo 35
5. Cooking Without a Recipe 42
6. If You've Seen One Mountain 53
7. The End Is in Sight. 73
8. Starting Over 85
9. The Master of Invention 97
10. Life Support 111
11. New Roles to Play 126
12. Lucky Accident 136
Epilogue 147
Acknowledgments 149
About the Authors 151

INTRODUCTION

My mother's life—which spans ninety-three years as of this writing—reads like a history book. I still marvel at some of her stories! Her life has in many ways been remarkable, and the lessons she's taken from it are unique and insightful. They're also surprisingly applicable to the challenges of today.

Together, my mother's experiences have contributed to one central, defining belief: There are no bad experiences in life, just the ones we don't learn from. She believes that if you can relabel your "bad" experiences, they will become valuable steps on your journey, helping you navigate the learning curve of your life. And let me tell you, she walks the talk and then some. As someone who has had the good fortune to hear her teachings over the years—though like any good daughter, I didn't always appreciate their true value at the time—I can tell you with confidence that she's right. And I'm not the only one who thinks so.

As an Action Coach, my goal is to help women discover what they want for themselves, to prioritize their own needs and desires. As I've found, women sometimes have trouble taking action because they simply don't know where they want to go. It's been so long since they've considered what they want or stepped back and evaluated their approach to life, often because they've been focused on caring for others.

In the course of my work and my life, I consistently find myself quoting my mother. Over and over, when sharing ideas and suggestions with the women around me, I hear myself repeating this phrase: "My mother always says . . ." That's because she not only had a lot of wisdom but also this extraordinary ability to boil her insights down to a single phrase or a sentence that's both memorable and effective.

Recently, I started including my mother among the speakers at my in-person events. Even though she's in her nineties, she stands on stage and confidently addresses audiences of more than one hundred women. Consistently, they are rapt by her stories and teachings. In fact she's the only speaker who always garners a standing ovation. I reasoned that if all these women are so moved and empowered by her lessons, why not share them with others?

Why does my mother's advice and insight resonate so strongly with people? In many ways, hers are the messages that we're missing in our lives. In today's world, which is so geared toward social media, most of our influencers are young people with a lot of flash. We've somehow lost the wisdom and acumen of the older generation. But there really are some lessons that require a lifetime of learning.

When we finally do hear them, words and advice from wise elders feel welcome and even comforting. They lend us a perspective that only comes with many years of history and experience. And they assure us that we, too, will be okay, that we can persevere, and that we can find meaning and purpose—and even fun—in the face of life's challenges.

Over the years, I, and now my own children, have received the benefit of my mother's insights and her hard-won wisdom, and now I'm happy to share them with you! Her story is truly one of always finding the silver lining.

Each of the chapters in this book opens with a narration of my mother's story—a piece of her life—told in her own words. It's followed by the lessons she learned from that time period. Then I jump in to provide my own take on the lessons. These include some of my personal experiences, as well as stories from a few of my clients. In some cases, a chapter includes a "Reprise," where one of the lessons discussed previously comes into play again, this time in a slightly different light.

As you read, I invite you to create your own takeaways and perspectives, as well. Just remember, there are no bad experiences!

Amy Goober

CHAPTER 1

How Lucky Can You Be?

"How does one become the luckiest woman in the world? Well, it helps if you're born in July 1931 in the middle of the worst depression in US history, and you're brought home from the hospital during a polio epidemic.

I know—it sounds like I'm being facetious, but I truly do know that I have been lucky because of my life's circumstances and not in spite of them. And it all started with my birth.

My mother, Minnie, returned home from the hospital with me to find that my four-year old-sister, Hilaire, had been diagnosed with polio. My frightened mother understandably shifted her attention to Hilaire, handing me off to her seventeen-year-old sister-in-law, Ruth, to care for me.

I'm told she put me in a carriage and wheeled me around like I was her little doll.

Meanwhile, my mother frantically tried to find volunteers to come to our Brooklyn, New York, home to help her perform an experimental polio treatment she'd heard about called the Kenny method, after Australian nurse Sister Elizabeth Kenny. Instead of the traditional metal leg braces, it prescribed rigorous, consistent movement of the child's limbs while they were submersed in warm bath water. And so, the Bathtub Brigade was created.

Luckily I was a hearty, healthy baby who thrived during those early months in the loving hands of the village of relatives who cared for me. Apparently I was cheerful and content, and my aunts and cousins loved playing with me. And I'm happy to report that the Bathtub Brigade was successful, and my equally lucky sister recovered full use of her limbs."

LESSONS LEARNED

#1: You can be parented by people other than your own parents

Gwen: When my sister contracted polio, my mother became consumed with trying to heal her. Of course she did! Even though I was a newborn, she simply didn't have time for me. The Bathtub Brigade took on a life of its own, and my needs were secondary. My aunt Ruth stepped in to help care for me as a parent would. I'm told that many of my father's sisters and in-laws visited our house and took over my needs as a newborn.

My mother wasn't able to nurse me as her milk dried up from the stress of caring for my sister. As a result I was truly one of the first bottle-fed babies, receiving my nourishment via anyone who was available. Family lore has it that I was "handed around like an hors d'oeuvre." I slept wherever and whenever it suited my caretakers. Interestingly enough, now I often say, "I can sleep on a fence post" because I'm able to sleep well anywhere. I became low maintenance out of necessity, and it has served me well.

The result was that I learned, from the youngest age possible, that whoever takes care of you is a parent.

Amy: I was so lucky to be born to the mother I had. She was always engaged and attentive. I have vivid memories of coming home from school each day and telling her every single thing that happened, always in chronological order! Now I realize how tedious that must have been sometimes, but my mother never showed it.

Both of my parents were actively involved in raising me, but my father died when I was fifteen. My mother always did an incredible job, first as a co-parent and then as a single parent. But while I sing her praises now, I didn't always appreciate her when I was growing up.

I had a best friend, Janet, in middle school whose mother knew how to sew and decorate cakes. I thought she was the best mother in the world! I asked my mom repeatedly why she couldn't be more like Janet's mom. My mom, in contrast, was an academic and very involved in community affairs. Now, as we write this book together and I learn more about my mom, I realize that what she had to give went well beyond what I could learn in any home economics class. And fortunately, I had Janet's mom to share those skills with me.

Just like no one person can be everything to another in a romantic relationship, no one parent can be all things to their child—including teaching them everything. It's okay, and necessary, to have more than one person to "parent" you.

Sometimes we focus so much on what we think we lack that we don't recognize what we have. This lesson can encourage you to take a few moments to appreciate and feel gratitude for those substitute parents or mentors who helped you get where you are.

> #2: *Every child in the family has a different set of parents*

Gwen: The polio diagnosis of my older sister, Hilaire, essentially reversed the typical birth order in our family because our parents had to pay so much extra attention to her. Fortunately she recovered, but Hilaire always was seen as a frail, sickly little kid who had to be taken care of. Essentially, I took on what would have been her role, becoming the strong, can-do older child even though, in reality, I was the younger one. I was never the baby, and she remained the baby. My parents were so focused on her that in many ways she became like an only child. My father was never around, and my mother—who was the youngest of six girls—was always looking to her sisters for help and advice on parenting.

The mother and father who parented Hilaire were doting and always concerned about her. They saw her as weak and frail. The mother and father who parented me expected me to be able to do everything on my own, take care of myself, and take care of my sister's needs as well. The anxiety around Hilaire's illness stayed with my parents well beyond her recovery, and so little was asked of her. She didn't have to perform any tasks or chores, while I often took up the slack in addition to doing my own housework. Although we were raised in the same home by the same mother and father, my sister and I most definitely had two different sets of parents—and that's okay. It was completely understandable given the circumstances of our early years.

Amy: I love that my mother can take such an open-minded view of what could have been a difficult or painful issue—the fact that she, by necessity, got so much less attention in her early years than her sister. As children and then as parents, we tend to think that everything should be "equal," but that's not realistic. If we can learn to understand that, we can save ourselves a lot of heartache.

In many ways it's natural to compare how our parents treated us to the way they treated our siblings. It's also normal to reflect on how differently you may have parented each of your own children. Each child in a family (unless they're twins) is born to or adopted by parents who are at a relatively different place in their lives—whether in their relationship with each other, their development as parents, or their own personal growth. Parents are (hopefully) constantly evolving and adapting as humans, just like the rest of us.

Though they were all parented by my husband, Bob, and me, each of my three children experienced us differently. Over the years some of our viewpoints and parenting skills changed and evolved.

We had our first baby, Samantha, when I was thirty-three. I had absolutely no experience with infants, and I couldn't believe the hospital actually let me take my brand-new daughter home! Bob and I read the baby books to each other, trying to figure out what this new being needed from us.

Three years later, when we brought home our son, Jimmy, he had more knowledgeable parents and also an older sister to add to the mix. As parents we quickly had to figure out how to manage two children simultaneously. Six years later, when we brought our last child, Jessie, home, it seemed she had more than two parents! Samantha was old enough to help care for her while Jimmy toughened her up as a big brother can. The age span of almost nine years from top to bottom gave Jessie parents who were almost a decade older and in some ways wiser than the ones Sam had!

Reflecting on this lesson can bring new insights

into your relationship with your parents and can shift how you view your own parenting. Think about the differences in the parents you had versus the ones your siblings had. Within the family you've created, take some time to recognize that you were naturally a different parent for each of the children who entered your family. Do you feel you were a "better" or "different" parent to one of your children over another? If so, that's okay! We live and, ideally, we learn.

CHAPTER 2

Alone in the Dark

"My good luck continued. I turned ten and Pearl Harbor was bombed! At the time, my father was in Norfolk, Virginia, scouting out housing for us for an impending move. He planned to start a new building business there. My perpetually frightened mother decided that we had to move sooner rather than later because she couldn't contemplate spending any time alone, without my father. So my parents packed up our family, our belongings, and our dog, and off we went to Norfolk.

When we arrived, our new house was far from ready. It was mid-December, and we moved in with no heat or electricity. Consequently, we slept in our winter clothing.

Once I was enrolled in school, we discovered that in addition to being exceptionally healthy, I was also three years *ahead of the other fifth graders in Norfolk. My parents decided against skipping me into middle school because I was still so young. Instead, my teacher set me to work painting murals in the halls of Emma Willard School, while doing my schoolwork independently. The school thought this would be a good way for me to pass the time while my classmates caught up to me.*

I remember loving my Girl Scout uniform because it made me feel like I was part of the war effort. I even learned first aid in case we were somehow needed.

At the end of the school day I walked home, and it was a very long way with no buses available. I sang to keep myself company. My parents somehow always managed to find a house the farthest distance possible from the school.

I wore a key around my neck to let myself in. Since everyone else worked during the war and my sister was focused on her dating life, there was no one home when I got there, which meant no one to clean the house. Guess who that duty fell to?

My mother liked a tidy home, and she expected me to keep the kitchen floor clean. She told me, "Don't use a mop—get on your hands and knees and scrub the floor with a sponge." Of course I hated it, but to pass the time I wrote poetry in my head, and I'd recite the poems to myself. I also made up stories where I was the main character. I imagined that I was Cinderella, and that all kinds of good things were going to happen to me.

Because of the war, the military had instituted all-night

blackouts to protect the area. There was great fear that the Nazis would bomb the local naval yards in Norfolk. There were no lights allowed in the windows, and no streetlamps. It was dark both outside and in! At night, as during the day, everyone was out of the house—everyone, that was, except for me. My mother was an air raid warden, and she took our dog out with her for protection. I guess she deemed me capable of protecting myself at the age of ten! My father had traveled to Texas to scout a new business there. And my sister was always out of the house with a busy social life. I was left alone in our pitch-black house for the long, seemingly endless nights. As I waited for dawn to come, I would tell myself tales about how I was heroically aiding the war effort, too. These stories gave me comfort and made me feel safe, and I believe that's what made me okay.

In the end, I learned to make up poems while scrubbing the kitchen floor. I honed my storytelling skills during those long, scary nights. What seemed like bad luck was really good luck because it made me strong and resilient."

⸙ LESSONS LEARNED ⸎

> *#3: You can learn how to parent yourself*

Gwen: The lonely days and nights in Norfolk when I was ten years old offered great opportunities for personal development and growth. I learned to comfort myself by having internal conversations. I learned to support myself with playacting in my head. Because I was alone so much, I guess you could say that I created a way to parent myself. I developed this skill out of necessity, and it's a powerful one to have. We don't always have the help and support of our parents or others, but that doesn't have to be a problem if we learn to offer love and care to ourselves.

The main job of parenting is to be responsive and attentive to your child's needs. To parent yourself, you have to look inside to discover what *you* need at that time. If it's support, give yourself support. Encourage yourself. Tell yourself that you're beautiful. Tell yourself that you're smart. And above all else, tell yourself you'll be all right. That's the most important part of parenting—to assure and reassure your children that all is well and everything will work out fine. Parents are there to give their children a sense of safety. When I was alone in the dark during those long nights, I kept telling myself that I would be okay and that I would be safe.

Being alone so much also afforded me a tremendous opportunity to read, which provided another source of support. Night after night I read in my bed with a flashlight under the covers because of the blackouts. Books introduced me to a whole other world—one filled with people who didn't exist in mine. Characters in books like *Little Women* were a window into what life could be like for other families. I pretended they were my family, and I learned a lot from them. That book gave me make-believe sisters who got along with each other, and a mother who was present. The March girls even had an absentee father, just like I did. While theirs was fighting in the war, mine was searching for business opportunities. Over the years, the characters in many books became the role models I didn't have.

Amy: We're never really taught how to parent ourselves. For me, the first time I had to learn that skill was when I went off to college. In those days, we called our parents once a week on Sunday to check in, and we wrote them letters. We didn't have the luxury of easily calling or texting them.

I have always leaned on my mother for big decisions. I remember calling her from college in tears, trying to decide whether or not I should go abroad for a semester. At the time, these trips were not the norm, and I had to join another college's program where I wouldn't know anyone else who was going. After many long conversations, I decided to venture to London. My mother chose to support me, but also ensured that I was making the decision on my own. While I could always count on her to be there for me, I was also learning how to look to and trust myself.

In my work with clients, I've seen that for some women, learning how to listen for and identify their own needs can be a huge challenge. They may never have realized that they can be the parent they need in difficult moments. When they start to master that skill, it's like a whole new kind of love and support becomes available to them.

As we reach midlife, many of us no longer have parents who are still alive. Women our age often feel especially alone as we realize we are, in a sense, orphans. My client Sarah, who was also a widow, felt this very deeply. Without the support of her own parents, she felt insecure and untethered. Together we created a few encouraging mantras, some of which were actual words or sayings from her parents. They were phrases like *I can do this*, *I am capable*, and *I'm not alone*. She put them on sticky notes around her house. When she was feeling low, these words of encouragement kept her going.

The next time you face a challenge or decision in your life, as you weigh and measure the options, be on the lookout for what your intuition is telling you. What do you know or feel in your gut? If you can flex this muscle of learning to consult yourself and be guided by your intuition, you'll see that you, too, can learn to support and parent yourself.

> **#4: There are no bad experiences in life, just the ones you don't learn from**

Gwen: Every day in Norfolk, in my preteen years, I came home to an empty house. In the evening, when he was in town, my father often brought home many of the men he worked with to have dinner with us. Because my mother was working full time, I became the chief cook and bottle washer in addition to my other housekeeping duties. It often fell to me to start preparing dinner for a big crowd. At the time, that did seem like a bad experience, but it was great training for when I'd have to feed a family of my own many years later! I actually learned how to cook, how to entertain people, and how to keep house.

From the outside, or for people who never lived through such experiences, it might seem like I had a tough childhood—that I had to endure a lot. To be sure, these challenges weren't easy, but they also weren't bad. That's because I was able to find value in them.

After those long days and nights, I learned that everything ends. No matter how long they may seem, the days end, and even the long nights, too. I also realized that, with the power of my imagination, I could turn something negative like scrubbing floors or coming home to an empty house into something positive. I created self-reliance. I didn't know it then, but that was a skill that I would need to call upon many years later.

All these experiences from my young life could easily be construed as bad because they were painful and scary to a young girl. But, in the end, they were valuable, although I didn't know it at the time. Like a lot of learning, it becomes muscle memory. The skills you assemble can help you when you need them later on. These experiences are rehearsals for life. And the more you use these skills, the more adept you are when it's your turn to star in your own show.

Amy: When I graduated from college, my best friend, Posy, and I moved to Boston to start our new lives and find jobs. It was 1981, and in many industries, women started out as secretaries. I was so anxious to actually get a job that I jumped at the chance to work in an advertising agency. It didn't take long for me to realize that I wasn't really *doing* anything—mostly just typing the letters my bosses wrote on their legal pads and answering their phones. I disliked the tasks of the job and constantly asked for more responsibility.

Four years of hard work and long hours went by, and I did reach the account executive level, but the old boys' network and the work itself were just not for me. I had a passion to succeed, but not there. That's when I realized that I could choose what I did and did not want to do. I ended up leaving the agency and starting my first business, opening a cake bakery in the Boston area. Even though the years in advertising were grueling and not very satisfying, they were what pushed me to leave and led me to have enough faith in myself and my abilities to start my first business.

We often overlook the lessons we can learn from challenging times. All we can think about is how "bad" things are. It's important to remember that while you can't change the experience, you can change how you frame it—how you view the impact it has on you and what you can learn from it.

In truth, without my years in advertising, I never would have opened The Icing on the Cake. The agency copywriter thought of the name, the art director created the logo, and the PR assistant got my first publicity in *The Boston Globe*.

> Looking back, you can acknowledge negative experiences, but also see the positives that can come out of them. Try to notice the beneficial traits you developed or lessons you learned. Hopefully you, too, can start to see that in some respects, there really are no bad experiences.

Reprise: You Can Be Parented By People Other Than Your Own Parents

Gwen: This theme of being parented by others continued throughout much of my life. As I was growing up, we moved around a lot. When I was ten and living in Norfolk, my mother went to work, and my older sister, now a teen and fully healed from polio, was out all the time. I came home from school with our house key tied to a string around my neck. The mothers in our neighborhood took me in after school—they were my substitute mothers.

These other women took me under their wings and taught me things. They gave me extra love and attention. They gave me little jobs, so I wasn't alone. I wanted to play the piano, so one of the women let me come over to use hers. I actually taught myself to read music. The woman next door taught me how to bake lemon meringue pies and would chat with me incessantly about her life. She was all of twenty-one, so she didn't seem that much older than I was, but she had two young children, and she taught me a lot about a life I didn't know firsthand.

I also found teachers all along the way who exposed me to books and opened my mind up to new ideas and even how to get along with other people. Teachers can be parent figures to many students.

I had my own mother, of course, but truly, she was like the cat who has kittens and drops them and never comes back. It was okay because I grew up knowing that there were always going to be people who took care of me. They mentored and cared for me in a way that my mother hadn't and couldn't. Just because my mother wasn't around, that didn't mean I wasn't cared for—I had other "parents" looking after me, and I thrived as a result.

Amy: In many ways, my mother was not really "parented" by her parents. She didn't feel supported by them as a child or even a teenager in any way other than financially. We can and should look at the silver linings in difficult circumstances, but it's also okay and sometimes important to acknowledge where our needs may not be met in life.

What I love about my mother's attitude is that she saw her own mother's shortcomings as simply part of her personality—they were not an indication of who my mother was as a child. Miraculously my mother managed not to internalize her mother's behavior, which is a reflection of her own incredible character. While I know what she experienced was hard, her attitude also allowed her to see the good that was present and be grateful for the people who did show up for her. There is a positive message in the negative modeling. My mom was able to say, *I'm not going to be the kind of mother I had.*

There are also times when your parent may not be there to parent you. My mother's uncle, Ben, who was my great uncle, also played a crucial role in my life. When I was twenty-five, I was considering opening up the bakery. Although my father was an entrepreneur who had run a thriving building business, he was no longer alive to counsel me. I spent many hours talking to Uncle Ben about my idea and trying to decide whether to take this big leap. Several years later, Uncle Ben was also the man who walked me down the aisle at my wedding, stepping in for my father, who couldn't fill that role.

Sometimes we become so fixated on the ways our parents or others in our lives weren't there for us that we overlook the spaces and places in which we *were* cared for. If you ever feel this way about a time or incident in your life, consider revisiting it with this approach in mind, seeking to identify who *was* present that supported you.

CHAPTER 3

More Than Just a Degree

"Opportunities for growth and development continued . . . When the war ended, we moved back to Brooklyn. As I entered high school, my father went to Ohio to build houses, and my sister went off to college in Virginia.

At school, I found that I was now three years behind my classmates. Not only was I having trouble with my spelling, I had a serious learning disability, though it was undiagnosed at the time. I was unable to pass either the standardized geometry or the intermediate algebra test, both of which were mandatory for graduation in New York.

But I was lucky once again! I had a prodigious memory, so I excelled in all other subjects and quickly caught up with my peers. The school chose to pass me in math. Apparently they decided that I was simply an idiot savant who got all A's in everything but math.

I discovered that I was only happy at school when I was NOT alone—perhaps because I'd been alone so much when I was younger. As a result, I joined everything I could find. I played all the women's sports and worked on the yearbook and the school newspaper, too.

With my father and sister away, my mother and I were left at home together, where we merely coexisted. She went to the movies and played cards while I was at school from 7:00 AM until 6:00 PM, busy with my activities. Looking back, I realize that I never really bonded with my mother. We didn't create that mother-daughter connection when I was a newborn or later during my school years. It's funny, but I never realized it until now, as I began recounting my experiences. The good thing about that is I didn't spend my life blaming her or feeling bad that she wasn't there for me. Eventually I found what I needed.

In January 1949, I managed to graduate from Tilden High School in just three and a half years. I was seventeen and, once again, found myself without any real adult guidance. My parents had always been hands off with me, so why should college selection be any different? I chose Bowling Green State University in Ohio based on its outstanding basketball team and its National Invitation Tournament chances.

As it turned out, my parents were leaving for a road

trip to California at the very same time I needed to be at college. Still, even though their itinerary took them right through Toledo, near where Bowling Green is located, they made no offer to bring me to college. I had no choice but to travel to college by train, alone. When I discovered that I had to change trains in Toledo at 2:00 AM for the connection to Bowling Green, I confessed to my father that I was a little frightened by the prospect. In his less-than-supportive way he informed me, "If you can't get there by train, then you're not ready to go away to college." Still, in a way he was right. So I did it, and gained some confidence as a result.

Once at Bowling Green, I felt like a fish out of water, so I transferred after just one semester. Upon my return home, I found out that my parents had bought a house in the middle of nowhere on Long Island. It was in a town called Massapequa, which was so small it didn't even have its own high school. I restarted college at nearby Hofstra University, where, to my immense delight and surprise, there was an excellent faculty, along with a sorority that wanted me as a member.

An adoring boyfriend who'd been attending Lehigh University transferred to Hofstra to be with me. I spent three years getting pinned, playing field hockey, and expanding my maturing brain. I did so well that I decided the boyfriend was now dull, and thus I chose a graduate school far away to escape the relationship.

That's how I ended up at the University of Michigan, where my excellent undergraduate training provided me with a quick transit through the master's program. At twenty-two, I finished my master's degree and headed home with a plan to marry a different man, a brilliant foreign student I'd met at Michigan. Not bad for a girl who couldn't spell or do math!"

 LESSONS LEARNED

> *#5: Who says you have to always be happy?*

Gwen: The US Constitution promises the right to *pursue* happiness; it doesn't guarantee that you'll experience it. I have reminded myself of this over and over throughout my life.

I picked Bowling Green for all the wrong reasons, thinking it would make me happy, which was a huge mistake. Who chooses a college based on their men's basketball team standings?

Getting there provided my first indication that my college experience was not going to center on happiness. There I was at seventeen years old, standing on an empty train platform at 2:00 AM, by myself with three pieces of matched luggage and no porters in sight. *I don't have to be happy,* I told myself. I was going to get to school somehow.

Bowling Green was a terrible fit for me, and I realized that pretty much right away. Yet I stayed and finished out the semester because it had been paid for. This was one of many times in my life that

I realized I needed to dig in and finish what I had started—happy or not.

Then, I chose to go home to New York and attend a nearby college. During my one semester away, my parents had decided to move from the city out to Long Island. I wasn't happy about that, either. On the ride out there I said to myself, *I knew they always hated me, and this proves it.* Yet although I was unhappy about my parents' move, it turned out to be a good thing. Landing at Hofstra was truly a lucky accident.

You don't have to be delighted or excited by a situation or a turn of events for it to have positive results. You just have to adapt and make the situation as good as it can possibly be.

Amy: What a relief to hear this lesson! We put so much focus on being happy, and it doesn't always happen. After my father died, I finished out high school. I applied to colleges and decided to attend Cornell. Although I was confident in my abilities in high school, I wasn't always confident in myself. My mother, now a single parent, packed me up and drove me all the way to Ithaca, New York. I was incredibly worried and anxious about the social aspect of college and whether I would or could fit in. After I settled into my dorm room, my roommate wasn't there yet, nor were many girls on my floor. When my mother was pulling away in the car, I said with tears in my eyes, "Thank you for leaving me in this unfriendly place."

That first year of college was so hard for me. It was fun in many ways, and I did make friends, but I thought seriously about transferring. Following college, I also wasn't happy in the advertising secretarial job.

Starting The Icing on the Cake from scratch and running it was also incredibly difficult! I can remember nights I came home and lay on the floor, crying to my husband that I couldn't continue. I did feel accomplished, but I wasn't always happy.

As this lesson reminds us, you don't always have to be happy. You can trade happiness for learning and growing. In all these situations I may not have consistently been happy, but I was gaining life experience, new skills, and self-confidence.

Sometimes dissatisfaction, irritation, disappointment, or any number of other "negative" emotions are what prompt us to make changes, either in our lives or the world around us. It's often our lack of happiness that causes us to seek new horizons—in other words, to grow. As such, not being happy can actually be just the push you need to improve your circumstances.

#6: Always have an exit strategy

Gwen: When you are facing a situation that makes you anxious, the best way to deal with it is to know that you don't have to put up with it; you can always get up and leave—that is, unless you're in prison. Some people struggle to realize that they don't have to get permission from anyone but themselves. You just have to make up your mind and do it.

When I was a freshman in college, I went on a blind date. I was only seventeen, and I had a lot of anxiety about going out with someone I really didn't know in a strange city. We went to the movies, and sure enough, I realized pretty quickly that I didn't like him. The thought of having to sit through the movie and then go out with him afterward was just awful. So I planned my exit. I said, "I'm going to the ladies' room," and I left my seat and never went back. I did often wonder how long he actually waited for me to return. But frankly I really didn't care. Maybe that wasn't the kindest choice in that moment, but that's where I'll lean on my youth. I was taking care of myself in the best way I knew how, and that was getting out of an unpleasant situation. So often women, especially, will stay in a place or with a person they know isn't right for them, simply out of a sense of having to be polite or not hurt anyone's feelings. Even when it's really better to leave.

I've had the same philosophy with relationships that I eventually knew were wrong for me. It seems I always had to have a boyfriend. When my current boyfriend decided to transfer to Hofstra to be near me, I felt a lot of pressure to stay with him because he had left his college to attend mine. He was a nice enough guy. But by the end of my senior year, I'd had an intellectual awakening, and so I was becoming bored with him.

I decided what I really should do was go to graduate school—far away! After that, the relationship dissolved on its own.

Having an exit strategy means you don't have to stay miserable and stuck, even if you're in a bad marriage or you have a husband who is abusing you.

It may take perseverance. For one, feeling trapped can paralyze your ability to think. Try asking yourself, *What's the worst thing that can happen if I* . . . fill in the blank. Don't be afraid of what other people are going to say or think.

Sometimes it can take hard work to find your way out, but there is a way, and it's worth it. *You're* worth it!

Amy: I think of this lesson more broadly, too—it's important to believe in yourself enough to know that you can always get out of any situation you're in that isn't positive.

I often view life in two columns: the things we can control and the things we can't control. As women, we often forget that we can steer many of our circumstances. There are definitely things in life that are givens that you can't control, like who you were born to, how tall you are, whether you have athletic ability, and so on. Yet there are many aspects of your world that are definitely within your control, but perhaps you've labeled them as givens.

One of my clients early in my career, Nancy, shared her very difficult story with me. She had been happily married (or so she thought) for fifteen years and had three children. She had recently discovered that her husband was not who he seemed to be. He was dishonest and using their savings to support a gambling habit. He had apparently been doing so for quite some time. The feelings of betrayal and rejection were overwhelming. Nancy struggled with how she would go on without her husband and the stability he provided. She worried about breaking up her family.

While we had to acknowledge all those fears

and feelings, we set to work creating some new ways for Nancy to build community and construct a new normal for her family structure without her husband. She did things like create different holiday rituals for herself and her children, and she made connections with other women in her area. In her case it wasn't the physical "exit" she needed help with because she had moved out. It was more of creating an "after exit" strategy to establish a better life for herself after she left.

Having an exit strategy is about recognizing when the situation is one you can control. But to leave—whether literally or metaphorically—you need to believe in your own ability to make that change happen. You need to know that you can get out of a bad situation. The first step is believing that you deserve to be living a good life. The next step is determining what you need to do to take action—where and how you can make your exit.

CHAPTER 4

Flying Solo

"Once home from college, I avoided seeking employment, but it found me anyway. On Labor Day, appropriately, my father informed me that I had to get a job. Following that, one morning he announced that he wouldn't leave the house to go to work unless I made some calls to local schools to try to get a teaching job. (While I graduated from Hofstra early, I had a double major in English and education, and a minor in history. Therefore, I was qualified to teach.)

I assured my father that by now the schools had already hired their staff for the school year. But he was adamant: three calls or he was going to stand over me all day long. The very first school I called, just five miles away, told me to come over immediately. They were trying to fill an opening for a first-grade teacher who had unceremoniously quit. I thought teaching young children was beneath my intellectual status, but I went and was promptly hired. I was furious that my newfound freedom had come to an end. Yet once again, I was actually lucky! It turned out that I loved being with those children so much that I could not believe they paid me to do it.

Instead of being bored, I learned a great deal while teaching first grade. For instance, I figured out that children would learn to read if the material was about them. So using the large-print Primary typewriter, I had each child dictate a short story of his or her life. I typed it, copied it, and produced a personal book for each child in my class. They loved it and learned to read it out loud to their parents.

I also devised a series of at-home visits to each child's family. At that time it was unheard of for teachers to learn about the child's home life. The parents were thrilled at my interest, and I learned more about "my" children by simply seeing where they slept, ate, and played. These experiences endeared me to the parents and taught me more than I could have learned had I instead taken yet another master's degree in education.

Initially I planned to save my money from my teaching job and marry my brilliant but poor student boyfriend from Michigan. But as fantasy was about to become reality, I changed my mind—I wanted to take my money and travel to Europe instead. I wrote an artful letter of apology to my *intended, and I took off for Paris. Traveling with my friend and then on my own turned out to be some of the most meaningful events of my life. It was a life-altering experience because I learned, for the first time, that I could be truly happy alone.*

Eventually after I returned, my brother-in-law introduced me to one of his clients. Seymour was a real estate developer who at thirty-one was good-looking and successful, and he drove a white convertible. I looked at my watch and found it was time to get married. In truth Seymour loved me very deeply, and I him. It was a match made in heaven. All the years of loneliness and adaptation to new surroundings and people combined to ready me for this next step. I felt like Cinderella, no longer washing the floors with a rag but finally finding her Prince Charming."

LESSONS LEARNED

> *#7: Spread your wings and learn to fly*

Gwen: My parents were so happy that I broke off my first engagement that when I asked them if I could travel to Europe, they let me go. No girl in my social class and at my educational level would have been permitted to go to Europe alone in 1953. But with my parents' approval, I planned to meet a college friend in Paris. I had the names of a few of my parents' friends who I could look up, along with five years of French under my belt. I was frightened as I made my way to the hotel on my own, but I ventured forth anyway!

What made me want so desperately to go was my education in literature. I felt like the Henry James character Daisy Miller exploring Europe. We got on trains and went to places like Biarritz and Madrid. I learned to grow outside of myself and see the world.

Before I left, my grandmother Sadie, who I adored, had become very sick. I was so conflicted because I didn't want to leave the amazing matriarch of our family. She counseled me, "I was the first person in our family to come to this country from Europe, and you are the first woman in our family to go back to Europe." Even though my grandmother was a very traditional and family-centric woman, she encouraged me to go because she had traveled to America alone at just fifteen. She was my lodestar, my inspiration. If she could do it, I felt that I could do it, too.

Amy: At sixty-three years old I created a women's travel group called Wandering Women, through which I've led many trips to various destinations. Now, I realize that this desire to repeatedly spread my wings has been a constant in my life. And I discovered that it dates all the way back to Grandma Sadie!

I've found a pattern among many of the women who consider traveling with me. In our initial conversations about possibly joining a trip, they often say, *This is way out of my comfort zone. I've never gone away with a group of women I don't know.* And I can empathize with that. Of course it's scary and uncomfortable. I often reply, "But what's the alternative? You can stay home and wonder what the world is like, what meeting new women would be like, and what you could be missing. Or you can take a leap of faith and push yourself beyond your comfort level."

What most of us need is just a gentle nudge to be able to convince ourselves to try something new, even if it's a little scary (or perhaps terrifying). It's like when your children want to dive into the pool for the first time, but they're a bit afraid. They stand there at the edge shaking, but all it would take is just a tap on their shoulder to get them to take that first dive.

One of my potential travelers, who we'll call Lucy, shared with me that she was incredibly uncertain about whether joining one of our trips was a real option for her. She was nervous and insecure about the whole idea, yet here she was, asking me for more information about the trip. She was torn between wanting to branch out and being afraid to do just that. I would never push anyone to do something she truly did not want to do, but I encouraged Lucy to give it a try. In the end, she joined us on our trip to Charleston, South Carolina. Afterward, Lucy said she was so happy she had taken the leap! It can be very empowering when you accomplish something that you thought was beyond your reach.

We can make a choice to either expand our world or contract it. When was the last time you stretched yourself outside of your comfort zone? Women of all ages can find their circles are shrinking, causing them to feel alone and lacking connections. If this is you, what can you do to open up your world? It doesn't have to be travel; it can be joining a book club or visiting a local coffee shop regularly. Small steps will lead to larger ones, and it's never too late to broaden your horizons.

CHAPTER 5

Cooking Without a Recipe

"I imagined that marriage would be like an extended honeymoon. I quickly learned otherwise. When my new husband was leaving for work, he stopped and asked me what time I would be home that night. He expected that we'd have dinner together. No one had paid attention to my whereabouts since I was fifteen. I realized then that the wings I had spread had now been clipped.

Although my husband thought that wives should not work, being married was not a full-time job for me. I decided to volunteer at the pediatric center at Long Island Jewish Hospital, helping children with leukemia. One day a week turned into four, and before long, I decided I wanted to return to paid work. This news was not well received. My *husband asserted that he required my time, and my father-in-law politely informed me that women in this family did not work. Keep in mind the year was 1957.*

I held my ground and returned to teaching, where I was welcomed warmly. However, in short order I was pregnant. In those days most women stopped working either when they became pregnant or when they started showing. Instead, I taught through my ninth month.

No one told me it hurt to deliver a baby, and at the first pang of pain, I rushed to the hospital. The admitting nurse broke it to me that I was not even in labor yet. I was so naive that I brought my portable Scrabble game, thinking I'd be playing while in labor.

Eventually I delivered our son, Bill. Then I decided I had better have another baby quickly, before I changed my mind about expanding our family. At nine months my son was not yet walking, so I figured, how hard could it be to have another? By the time my beautiful daughter, Amy, was born, Billy was running and climbing, and I understood why women spaced out their babies.

During this time, we moved back to Long Island, into the family home I'd resisted so many years before. But this time, life was good. I learned on my own how to be an attentive, interested mother. I joined the school's PTA and became a Cub Scout den mother. I could have earned a PhD in suburban motherhood!

My parents had moved to Florida and spent much of

their time off seeing the world, so I had to enlist help elsewhere. With my husband's seven-day work week, I knew I needed support!

A wonderful Swedish woman, Elsie, became the second-in-command at baby central, and I continued to rely on the kindness of others. We spent our weekends with my neighbor, Noel, who had five children of her own and a large, loving family . . . just like Little Women. *It struck me that my previous experiences reading* Little Women *as a child set the stage for what would come later, and this was a pattern that would repeat throughout my life."*

LESSONS LEARNED

> *#8: The last free breath is on the delivery table*

Gwen: When my children were young, I was offered a graduate fellowship toward a PhD. I was a stay-at-home mom at the time, and I started pursuing the coursework. Simultaneously my oldest, Bill, started stuttering. I reached out to a psychologist for advice, and he told me that all I needed to do was stay home and spend more time with my son. I was conflicted because one of my personal goals had always been to get my PhD while still in my twenties. But he was my son, and he needed me. When I went to the graduate school department head to inform her that I was going to leave the program, she said, "Mrs. Schwartz, you're being manipulated by your child." It was one of many pieces of unsolicited and unwanted advice I would receive as a parent. In the end, I gave up the PhD opportunity. It's hard to do something for yourself when your child has great needs. Yet sure enough, within months Bill stopped stuttering, so it was a successful intervention.

With the bond that's formed when the baby is in utero, mother and baby are one. Even when the umbilical cord is cut, there always remains a symbolic bond. The time when you can think primarily about yourself ends with the birth of your first child. It's the last time you can say, *This is what I want*, without regard for another person. Mothers are not "free" to move through the rest of their lives without considering their children and their needs. This is something we don't realize until we have a child. We couldn't possibly. As mothers, we don't always *want* to recognize it.

After you give birth, that small being occupies most of your thoughts. Even when they're fully grown, your children's needs are your needs. If your child falls and gets a cut, you bleed also. That's simply the way it is. It's not always easy to live with, but it's true.

Amy: There was a time in my married life when I wasn't sure that I wanted to have children. I couldn't imagine bringing a baby into the world as it was. That was in the late 1980s, and it was actually the AIDS epidemic that led to this feeling. Not wanting to bring a baby into our current world is a refrain many women also say today.

Not long after I made this announcement, during a walk on the beach with my mother, she said, "You should at least have one child so you can learn what real love is." I took her advice to heart and went on to have three children of my own.

It can sound like a difficult thing, this idea of no longer being "free," but it's absolutely worth the trade-off. For me, raising my children and being a parent has been one of the true joys of my life. Now I understand that the love for a child is the highest level of love.

I don't think there's any way to explain what it's like to be a parent and how your life can be so affected by having a child—how it reorganizes you and your priorities. You understand it when you experience it.

When I became a mother, I immersed myself in my children in a way I might never have expected. Parenting was certainly difficult at times and not for the faint of heart. Yet the years flew by, and sooner than I anticipated, it came time for my children to leave for college and, beyond that, to live life as adults. It can be challenging when your children grow up. It's almost as if we want them to be as dedicated to us as we once were to them. The connection I felt for my children was very strong, but I knew they were off to live their own lives. If you do your job as a parent, your kids should be able to separate from you successfully and even fearlessly.

That's when I decided to focus on helping midlife women and empty nesters through this transition. I created programs to connect women at this stage of life and developed opportunities for them to learn, be inspired, and travel—all this so I wouldn't cling too tightly to my own children!

As parents—and especially as mothers—we worry about and stay deeply connected to our children from the moment they are born. In a sense you will never be totally "free" of your children, nor would you want to be, but eventually you will regain some of your time and energy. And you get to decide what to do with it! It doesn't have to be a big, life-changing undertaking. You can simply discover new hobbies, relationships, or interests that enrich your own life.

#9: Don't be afraid to fail

Gwen: In 1957, the Russians launched their Sputnik satellite, and the United States government and its agencies began to fear that we would be left behind in the space race. As a result, many new educational programs were started in those subsequent years. In the early 1960s, as I was home with two very young children, I received a call from my local school principal. "Gwen," he said, "we have a problem. We've started a program for gifted children in our elementary school. The math teacher has become ill, and we'd like you to fill in for her two days a week."

Me? I thought. *I failed geometry and algebra!* Still, it sounded like a good way to get back into the field and, quite frankly, to get out of the house for a bit. So I agreed.

I reasoned that all I had to do was stay a page or two ahead of the kids, because they had no way of knowing what lay ahead, either. Admittedly, this took a bit of magical thinking on my part. Just as I did when I was a child in Virginia, I simply told myself that everything would work out.

Using my "worst-case scenario" method, I realized that in the event that the job didn't pan out, I would just be back at home where I was happy anyway. After I had been working for about two weeks, the principal came into my classroom. "Oh," he said casually, "I forgot to tell you that there's a district-wide one-day workshop explaining our new gifted program. You'll have to do a presentation to show everyone what we're doing in math and science."

I said, "You must be kidding. I just got here!"

"You can do it!" he said.

Well, I thought, *I'm fast on my feet. The presentation is only two hours—I can figure it out.* Later, as I got ready to give my talk, I looked around the room and realized that no one in the audience knew more than I did. And I decided right then and there that I was not afraid to fail.

I tap-danced my way through, adding a few jokes here and there. At the end of the session, a gentleman came up to me and said, "My name is Robert. I'm the supervisor of education for gifted children for the state of New York, and I loved your presentation. I want to offer you a job supervising the elementary school program for the gifted for the state of New York." I was flattered but had to decline because I couldn't make the required move to Albany.

That experience reinforced my belief that we really don't know how much other people know.

Often, they know less than we do, so we shouldn't be afraid to go out there and do our best. Maybe we'll fail, but maybe we'll win!

Amy: Perhaps I inherited this bravery from my mom, but when I was just twenty-six years old, I started my first business. After four years clawing my way up from a secretarial role to an account executive title at the advertising agency, I was done. Once I got where I said I wanted to be, I changed my mind and decided that advertising wasn't for me.

As a child I had loved cake decorating and continued this hobby into my teens and twenties. I took and then taught cake decorating classes, always bringing my "homework" into the ad agency coffee room. "You should open a bakery!" my coworkers urged me. So although I had no business or bakery experience, I did just that!

If at any point I had seriously looked at the competition, the market, or the profit potential, I would have changed my mind. But I was undeterred. I just kept putting one foot in front of the other, and in 1986, I opened The Icing on the Cake in Newton, Massachusetts. It was a grueling undertaking, and it seemed I learned many lessons the hard way.

In those years, I was often nervous about what

would happen and whether the bakery, and I, would be a success. Would the brides like their wedding cakes? Would the New England Aquarium praise the cake we made for their twentieth anniversary, serving a thousand people? Would I be able to keep my employees? To me, a better title for this lesson is *Be afraid, but do it anyway.*

What is on your list of things to do that falls outside your comfort zone? What have you been talking about doing for a long time, but have never gotten around to? If you don't have a list, I suggest you make one. Your goals can be small, medium, or large. You don't have to start a business. You can learn something new, participate in a new activity, or join a new group.

If you find that you *are* afraid to fail, do it anyway! That's the point: Don't let your fear get in the way of moving forward. Just ask yourself, *What's the worst thing that could happen?*

CHAPTER 6

If You've Seen One Mountain

"As the kids got older, Seymour shifted his business life and finally decided to slow down. He was able to take off the whole summer, so I decided it was time for us to travel. I planned a summer-long road trip across the US to a host of national parks, even including tennis camp in Montana for the children.

Was everyone happy? Not on your life. My son was thrilled to go out West. I had invited my niece Cathy, and she was similarly excited. Amy wanted to stay home with her friends. But we went anyway. We packed ourselves in the station wagon, armed with travel brochures and hotel guides. In the back seat, the three adolescents argued constantly over who had to sit in the middle spot.

To pass the long hours, and without the electronic devices

of today, I decided we were going to read our way across the country. We took turns reading aloud from books including Bury My Heart at Wounded Knee, Last of the Buffalo, *and* Travels with Charley. *My literature selections only appealed to the adults. However, I learned that my husband was a fantastic traveler. Not only was he an expert driver, he was a fearless explorer.*

For her part, Amy had little interest in the national parks, and she hated tennis camp. I imagine she cursed the day she was born to a mother like me, just as I'd done at times as a child. But I had the time of my life, and my husband loved it so much he started planning a trip to Canada for the following year."

⁕ LESSONS LEARNED ⁕

> *#10: Travel is the true test*

Gwen: My husband, Seymour, did all the driving on our cross-country trip. One day, we crossed the Rocky Mountains via Loveland Pass, an extremely steep twelve-thousand-foot, two-lane mountain road. The trucks creeping upward ahead of us carried huge loads. We couldn't pass because of the narrow hairpin turns.

As we reached the crest of Loveland Pass, our carburetor failed, and we had no power. There was an incredibly sharp drop to our right with no fences or guardrails. Seymour, who had never dealt with such a situation, had the expertise to quickly find a little place on the road just wide enough for us to glide onto. This was a time with no cell phones, so we had to entertain ourselves while we nervously waited. Fortunately, the engine finally came back to life again.

Throughout the situation, Seymour stayed calm, had great patience, and never lost his temper. I really saw his true character as he took care of his family in a challenging situation. This incident validated and reconfirmed my belief that Seymour was a wonderful person.

With travel, all kinds of unexpected things can happen. You may face difficult or demanding circumstances, so good aspects of someone's character can come to light. Traveling with someone can show you whether you can get along with one another. It can reveal whether you can respect each other's feelings. And it can demonstrate whether you have the patience to put up with unexpected events.

Amy: While it's true that travel can be a test of a romantic relationship, it can also be another type of test. Until recently, I traveled for fun and adventure. I'd travel with friends, my family, or my husband for all kinds of occasions and events, or just because. I've always enjoyed it and found it to be a big highlight in my life!

A few years ago, I had been coaching women to take action with my Drive Your Life program. It was a virtual program, but someone asked if I'd create an in-person women's retreat. I had never imagined anything like that, but when the idea came up, I thought, *Yes, I can do that!* For the first retreat, I chose Scottsdale, Arizona, and jumped into planning the event. The result was an amazing experience for the seven women who joined me.

Since then, I've led women's trips to many destinations, including Charleston, South Carolina; St. Augustine, Florida; San Juan, Puerto Rico; Lake George, New York; Savannah, Georgia; Cancún, Mexico . . . The list goes on!

For me, travel is now a different kind of test. It's a test of creating great experiences and opportunities for women. And it's a test for those who join me as strangers to put faith in the process. Travel also has become a test of expanding boundaries and comfort zones. The women who travel with me are unsure what the experience and the other women will be like. That's a given. But they also don't know if they'll be comfortable or even glad they came along.

Travel has also become a big test of my ability to choose the right locations, the best hotels, and the most desirable excursions and activities. It's a test of my endurance and resiliency. It's also a test of whether I can bring women together and whether I can nudge them to get out of their own day-to-day lives and take a leap of faith!

Looking back at the national parks trip, maybe one of the reasons I didn't enjoy it is that I had no input in the planning or the decision of where to go. Yet perhaps that frustration helped to inspire me to do what I'm doing today, which requires me to take total control of the planning. Maybe this is another example of finding the silver lining.

#11: One man's meat is another man's cholesterol

Gwen: On our cross-country trip, we had Bill (13), Amy (12), and our niece Cathy (13) in tow. I was determined to show the children the raw beauty of the national parks and the important history of our country. I chose to read them historically accurate books to inspire an interest in travel and our nation's past.

When we arrived at one of the many parks on our itinerary, Amy refused to get out of the car. She declared, "If you've seen one mountain, you've seen them all!" Quite a comment to hear while we were focused on sharing our country's majestic beauty. In that moment, I learned that what I saw as an incredible and worthwhile experience was completely unimportant and boring to her.

It's critical to remember that perception is reality. We must acknowledge that everyone is different, and we may not agree with their choices. We usually lack the same frame of reference, and there's not just one truth. Amy's perspective was just as true for her as mine was for me.

This rule is important to remember when you find yourself criticizing other people's choices and views. There don't have to be reasons why others think differently or choose other options. It can merely be that what you find positive, they find negative. What's satisfying or enjoyable to one person can be disappointing or flat-out misery-inducing to another.

Amy: While writing this book with my mom, who I have always been close to, I've realized that we certainly have plenty of differences. She was much more of an academic than I was. Even though I went to a good college and did well, I've never been driven to learn in the way that she has. She's always been interested in the world around her, including politics and current affairs. I, on the other hand, am more insular. I focus more on my circle and my life than on what's happening in the world. She's always watching the news, and I never turn on the news. My mother reads very challenging books and literature, and I'm more of a beach-read person. She's an adventurous and dedicated cook still making a full dinner each night at ninety-three years old. While I enjoy cooking, I take shortcuts and am easily persuaded to eat out or order in. We had very different upbringings and different experiences in our marriages and as parents.

The list goes on and on, yet as different as we are, I always find myself quoting my mother's wisdom! And here we are writing this book together. The fact that I value her beliefs and want to share them shows that underneath it all, my mother and I actually have some deeper things in common. As I age, I have come to appreciate our similarities more than our differences.

Left: Gwen and her big sister Hilaire, 1933. Below: Gwen, 1950.

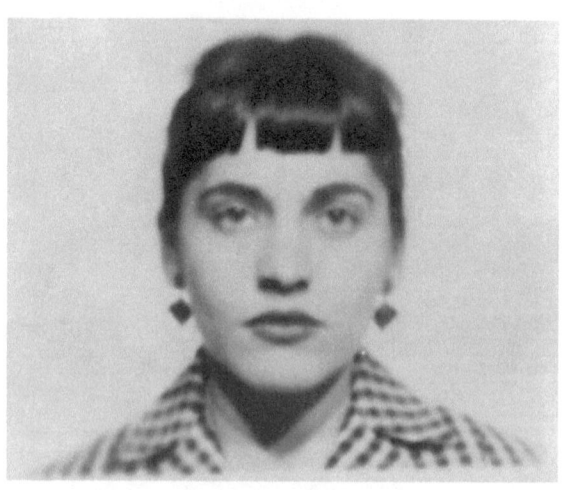

*Left: Gwen,
Hofstra University
graduation, 1952.
Below: Gwen,
Elementary School
Teacher, 1958.*

Gwen and Seymour's wedding, 1956.

Above: Gwen's parents, Minnie and Milton, at Gwen's wedding, 1956. Below: Amy, 1959.

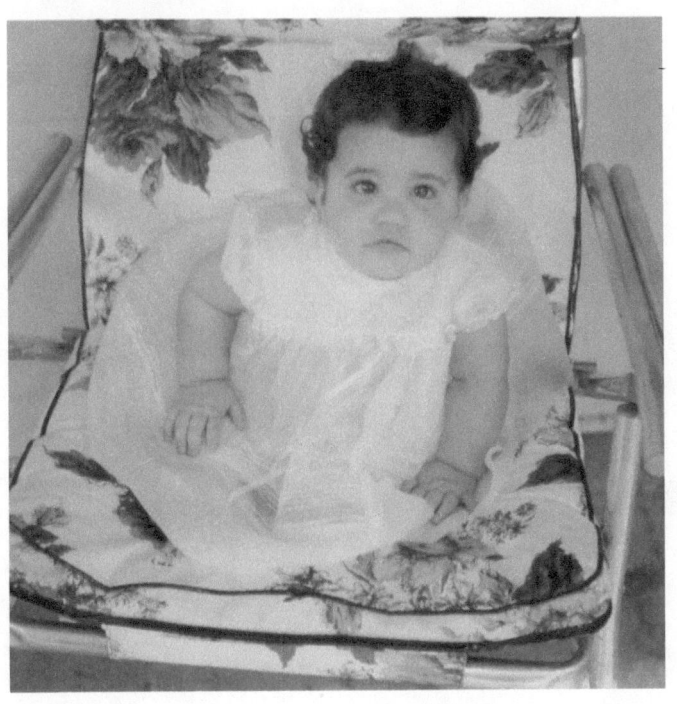

Left: Amy with Seymour, 1964. Below: Gwen, Bill, and Amy, 1963.

Above: Gwen, Seymour, Amy, and Bill, 1964. Left: Gwen, Seymour, and Amy, 1971.

Above: Gwen, Seymour, Bill, and Amy at Bill's Bar Mitzvah, 1974. Below: Gwen and George, 1977.

Gwen traveling, 1979.

Amy and The Icing on the Cake, 1986.

Uncle Ben walking Amy down the aisle, 1987.

Gwen and Samantha, Long Island, 1997.

Left: Gwen traveling, 1987. Below: Gwen's grandchildren: Samantha, Jimmy, and Jessie, 2001.

Left: Gwen, George, Samantha, Jimmy and Jessie, 2005.
Below: Samantha and Chris' Wedding, 2021: Jimmy, George, Gwen, Samantha, Amy, Bob, and Jessie.

CHAPTER 7

The End Is in Sight

"Now time shifts forward rapidly. The clouds are gathering. In 1972, my mother died, followed by my father a year later. I realized that suddenly, I was an orphan. I hadn't had the most present or supportive parents, but being without them still had a profound impact on me. The next July, in 1974, we sent the children to summer programs. I had a hysterectomy with a quick three-week recovery. Then Seymour and I went off to Canada alone to enjoy a second honeymoon.

One day in September, Seymour came home from a tennis match and said he was having trouble seeing the ball crossing the net. He quickly went to the ophthalmologist and from there was referred to a neurologist. To demonstrate just how "fine" he was, Seymour drove himself into Manhattan to see the doctor. But as we waited many days for the neurologist's follow-up call, it seemed that perhaps he couldn't bring himself to tell us what he really suspected.

On October 12, I drove Seymour to the emergency room so he could be seen by a local doctor and receive medical attention. They admitted him. The chief of neurology took me aside and told me the news was very bad. They discovered that Seymour had a dumbbell-shaped tumor behind his eyes that was so large that surgery to remove it would take most of his brain. He told me that, benign or malignant, this tumor would kill my husband within a matter of months. Straight talk, indeed.

I asked the neurologist if I could bring my children to his office so they could hear the prognosis directly from him. I prepped my son and daughter that we were going to hear bad news, but we had to know the truth. Amy thought to bring a handkerchief. The doctor told my children, "Don't pray for your father to live long . . . He will go blind and not be able to understand anything." It turned out that the doctor was the one who needed the handkerchief. And with that, we three went home to prepare for the worst.

At 7:00 AM the next morning, Seymour called and said, "Get me out of here." They had taken him down for radiation without informing his neurologist. My husband didn't understand what was happening, and he wanted to leave the hospital. Against doctor's orders, I made the decision to take him home. Shortly after, he fell and landed back in the hospital.

I spent hours on the phone trying to find ways to help Seymour, but countless doctors told me they didn't know anything else to do for him. I realized that if we couldn't save my husband's life, we would try to give him the best and most peaceful death possible.

I decided not to tell my husband that he was dying. I felt that as his reasoning and presence of mind had deteriorated, he really couldn't understand what was happening anyway. There was no point in him feeling anxious and scared. We were in the hospital day and night. The children were doing their homework in his room while we all played "let's pretend."

When Seymour was no longer able to walk, I had to arrange for nurses around the clock to care for him. Meanwhile, I tried to guide my children through the emotional horror of what was unfolding. Yet I had no idea how to deal with the business part of this ordeal. Seymour was a lone wolf in his business dealings—there was no one else who knew everything. He had a stable of real estate lawyers and an accountant he worked with, yet mostly he functioned alone. At one point the accountant called to tell me he had arranged a meeting of all these people so they could direct me in running my husband's business.

Our lawyer informed me that my brilliant husband had

to be declared incompetent for me to be able to take over. Yet ironically, he had to be "of sound mind" to sign the papers. None of these professionals was willing to help me navigate that process. And I cried all the way home.

Having no family to turn to, I called my best friend, Harriett, who told me she had a good friend, George Borden, who was a lawyer in our town. He was very smart and might be able to help. I followed her advice, and George actually suggested that all I needed was a power of attorney. He miraculously offered that if Seymour had a lucid moment, he would come to the hospital and get the papers signed.

In a stroke of luck, Seymour had a moment of clarity, and I called George. Sure enough, he rushed to the hospital with the paperwork, which my husband was able to sign. George, in an act of great compassion and kindness, solved this problem quickly, painlessly, and efficiently. Then, after I said thank you, he seemed to disappear just as quickly as he'd come.

The standard procedure at the time would have been to put my husband in a nursing home to live out his final days. Despite dire warnings from my doctor and well-meaning friends, I decided to have my husband die at home. Meanwhile, I worked to turn our home into a hospice. In those days, that was something that was rarely, if ever, done. Amy gave up her first-floor bedroom for the cause. We brought in nurses around the clock so Seymour could be in his own house, around his wife and children, for the remainder of his life.

During the holidays, we had little to no family support with my sister and sister-in-law busy taking vacations with their families.

On a snowy February morning, the nurse on duty arrived, and the children went off to school. I went into the kitchen to make Seymour one of his favorite foods. Before I finished cooking, the nurse came in to tell me that he had simply stopped breathing. As per his wishes, we decided to donate his body to NYU Medical School for brain tumor research.

I sat with Seymour a few minutes, then kissed him goodbye. When Bill and Amy walked home from school, I greeted them at the door and told them that their father had just died. With the deaths of my father, my mother, and my husband coming in such close succession, I was in the perfect storm of grief and loss."

 LESSONS LEARNED

> *#12: Happiness is like pigs rolling in the mud, not knowing that tomorrow they'll be bacon*

Gwen: In the fall of 1974, Seymour and I were in our sunny halcyon days. We had no idea that the guillotine was about to fall. It was a time when everything felt perfect. We had returned from a wonderful trip, our children were doing well, and we were getting ready to think about them going off to college. Life was good. It was like pigs rolling happily in the mud, not knowing what would befall them in the days to come. In the blink of an eye—figuratively and literally—everything changed.

Happiness is, in many ways, a state of ignorance. It requires a refusal to acknowledge the world as it is, with all its challenges and obstacles.

Being unhappy is simply understanding the human condition, and acknowledging the fact that there are dangers all around you in life. Happiness is wonderful, but it's a limited state of being. You can be happy only for short periods of time. Otherwise, you'd just be playing dumb. You'd have to tune out reality.

Yet it's also important not to be anxious all the time about what might happen. Be aware that whatever challenges are ahead, you will be able to deal with them. You don't want to die twice—once anticipating death and then a second time when it actually happens. You shouldn't "what if" yourself your whole life. Doing that will rob you of the joy you can find.

And even after you've been in the worst place in your life—when you've experienced the most terrible thing you can imagine—it's comforting to know that everything passes. When it does, you can experience happiness again.

Amy: As someone who experienced unexpected tragedy early in my life, I find that sometimes when things are going well, I worry that danger is ahead. My mind searches for what could go wrong. People often ask me what it was like to lose a parent at such a young age. I can tell you that it was horrible. I was only fifteen, but at the time fifteen didn't feel young. I was as old as I had ever been. Looking back, I was really just a kid. It was only when each of my own children turned fifteen that I truly realized just how young I was when my father died.

At the time I was part of a big group of girlfriends. When I found out that my father had a brain tumor, my mother told me to keep it to myself. She had decided not to tell my father he was dying because in all honesty, he really wasn't aware of what was happening. To that end, she didn't want it talked about outside of our house. It was like keeping the worst kind of secret. I had to continue on as if everything was okay, yet it was anything but.

My so-called friends pretty much dropped me from the group because I didn't go out and wasn't "fun" anymore. Girls can be so cruel, and I learned that firsthand. It was like suffering on top of suffering, and overall it was a terribly lonely time for me.

I think the finality of my father's death didn't really hit me at the time. I was the only person I knew in my very large high school whose father had died. That in and of itself was very isolating. After only a few days, I went back to high school with all its pressures and my insecurities, and just had to continue along. Having experienced that kind of struggle so early in life was especially hard.

For me this lesson is about enjoying your happiness when you find it, and not obsessing about what could spoil it. Living in the moment is one way to do that. Try to be truly present and appreciate life's good moments instead of waiting for the axe to fall. Stop and really feel the joy—soak it in. Go ahead and be that pig rolling in the mud, no matter how temporary it may be!

For most of our lives, we focus on finding happiness. But even when we do find it, no one stays happy all the time. It's important to recognize and acknowledge that things can and will happen to disrupt your happiness. That's simply part of life. You have to settle for a measure of acceptance and understanding of the forces that rule our lives because to fight them is just wasted energy, and it spoils the happiness you do feel.

#13: We often worry about the wrong things

Gwen: I think we all worry about the wrong things. We spend so much energy fretting over small things that are never going to harm us. The terrible thing that's awaiting us could be hiding in plain sight, and we just haven't seen it yet.

My husband, Seymour, was the healthiest person I could have imagined. He was forty-nine and fit, and he ran his own business and was in the prime of his life. I never would have dreamed that this man who never smoked, who was an athlete, and who didn't have a sick day in his life was going to be dead before he turned fifty. Of all the things I worried about, that was not one of them.

At the same time, if I had spent our years together worrying about Seymour dying young, I would have missed out on so many happy memories with my family. I could have worried about many things that would have changed my life, but what good would that have done?

Not only do we often worry about the wrong things, but worry itself is a waste of time and energy. Pay attention to the things that require concern, of course, but don't worry about the rest. If your child is sick, take him to the doctor. But don't worry about your child at some point possibly getting sick. Try to focus on what's actually happening, and don't fret over anything and everything that *could* happen. Spending time on "what if" is counterproductive.

Amy: I am a worrier. It can become a habit that's difficult to break. Sometimes, it feels like if we just worry enough, it will somehow prevent bad things from happening. But the fact is, we can't prevent what we don't even know is coming.

Intellectually, I know that worrying is counterproductive. It gives the illusion of control because we think we're "doing something." But what we obsess about is, in most cases, unlikely to happen. Inevitably, the future will look different from what we anticipate. Plus, oftentimes when something truly bad does occur, people actually tend to recover relatively quickly. We anticipate that we won't be able to handle things, or that they'll be worse than they actually are, but we're stronger and more resilient than we think.

When worry overtakes your thoughts, try to consciously focus on something positive. Maybe it's a good memory or a place that brings you joy. Or perhaps devise a mantra to reassure yourself of your own resilience, like *I can handle it. I'll be okay.* Or borrow my mother's phrase, *Everything will be all right.*

There are also some action steps you can take when worry overcomes you. First, write about it. Take a few minutes to write down all the things you're worried about. This action, by itself, can decrease your anxiety.

Second, ask yourself if there's anything you can do about these worries. If you're worried about a physical symptom you're having, call and make a doctor's appointment. If you're worried about a financial issue, take a long look at your finances or get some help or advice. There is usually something you can do to diminish your concerns. If there is absolutely nothing you can do about it, then you'll have to accept that and try to let the worry go.

A third technique that I learned recently is to picture a river flowing past you, and put your worries into the river. Picture them floating away from you. These steps can help you decrease your worrying and help you feel more in control.

CHAPTER 8

Starting Over

"The long period of the death watch had ended quietly, and I was left wondering, Now what? I was no one's child, no one's wife, and no one's lover. Both of my children were preparing to apply to college, and I was unemployed. For the remainder of the year, I worked part time at the local high school, teaching. I also sold some of my husband's real estate holdings and tried to get used to this new period of changing roles.

I started talking to myself, as I'd done when I was a child. I reminded myself that I was safe and that everything would be okay.

Recalling that one of my happiest roles was as a student, I decided to return to school. While my children were applying to college, I was applying to social work school and law school. The former accepted me immediately. Law school wait-listed me, so that made the decision easy. Social work it was! I went directly to Adelphi University School of Social Work. By 1975, my son was at Harvard, and by 1977, my daughter was starting at Cornell, and I was headed to social work school. All three of us off on our academic adventures!

Meanwhile, George Borden, the lawyer who rescued me from a difficult situation when my husband was dying, had come back into my life. I remembered he had never sent me a bill for his legal services. Every other lawyer that I worked with during that period—and there were many—sent a bill, swiftly and without fail. So when I realized this, I wrote George a letter thanking him and reminding him that I had never received a bill and would like him to send one along. He immediately replied that he was not going to charge me and that my thank-you was enough payment.

As New Year's Eve 1976 approached, I decided that I wanted to thank all my friends for their enormous support during Seymour's illness. So I resumed my old habit of throwing a New Year's Day open house party. I remembered George's kindness and decided to invite him along with the others who'd helped me so very much. I also had an ulterior motive. I planned to set George up with one of my divorced friends by asking him to drive her home after the party.

George came to the party, and sure enough he agreed to drive my friend home when I asked him. Then he promptly returned to spend more time with me! After that, he really never left. He became a fixture in my life from that time on.

LESSONS LEARNED

> #14: Learn to ask for help

Gwen: The news that I needed to declare my dying husband incompetent, so that I could manage his business and file our income taxes, was devastating. Not only did I see him as a brilliant businessman, but I had no idea how to go about that process.

My friend Harriett thought that George would be able to help me, and she also knew his wife had recently died, so she felt he would be sympathetic. Fortunately, she was right on both counts.

For most of my life, my job had been learning to take care of myself, then my children. Suddenly I had the new challenge of taking care of a very sick man and learning to run a business I knew nothing about.

So I asked for help, and it was immediately granted. Thank goodness. I'd grown accustomed to knowing what I was doing at home and in the classroom. It was a humbling experience to realize how little I knew of the rest of the real world. My friends knew I needed help without my asking. Each night a home-cooked dinner arrived at our house and someone appeared to drive Bill, Amy, and me to the hospital to visit Seymour and then bring us back home.

Often people don't ask for help because they're embarrassed about their own failings. You may experience fear of rejection or worry that the help will not be given. But sometimes, the only way forward is with the assistance of others, and you've got to go into that uncomfortable space of admitting you need help, then asking for it.

Amy: Asking for help comes naturally to some and not to others. I encourage the women in my world always to reach out for help because we just can't go it alone in this life.

Thirty-eight years ago, I was approaching the date of my wedding to Bob—in July 1987. I was living in Massachusetts, but I had grown up on Long Island, and that's where our wedding was being held. My mom had done a lot of the heavy lifting in terms of the planning as I was engulfed in the bakery.

Bob's mother, Lillian, had been sick for about nine years with emphysema, a result of decades of cigarette smoking. Her health seriously declined as our wedding date approached. Sadly she died at the end of April that year, and it was a very sorrowful and devastating time—not just for us but for Bob's father, Harold, as well.

Harold was a sweet man—a World War II veteran who ran his own small accounting business in Sharon, Massachusetts. He had gone from living in his parents' house right into the military. He then married Lillian, and they moved into their own house. Harold's basic needs had always been taken care of by someone else. During the time Lillian was in the hospital and after she died, he sank into despair and, we later realized, depression.

I remember going to his house, where Bob and I tried to teach him the basics of cooking. Bob's brother, Joel, and his wife, Karen, helped as much as they could. Harold's brother, Mel, gave support from a town nearby. But Harold still struggled to care for himself and deal with his grief.

Bob and I got married on a Saturday, and the following day we went to be with our visiting out-of-town family. That afternoon we received a call from Joel that Harold had suffered an emotional breakdown during his attempt to drive back to Massachusetts from New York. He wasn't able to drive his car, and he had basically shut down emotionally.

He must have held it all together just long enough to get through the wedding. Of course we were aware that Harold was facing challenges, but because he didn't want to, or maybe didn't know how to, ask for help, none of us really understood the severity of what was happening.

I know that women often don't ask for help because we think we can do it all. As natural multitaskers, we take on everything and assure ourselves that we can do the juggling act. Or perhaps we feel like we don't want to burden others with our needs.

But it's not a weakness to ask for help—just the opposite. Asking for help can be a sign of strength, an understanding that you're human. I hope you'll decide to reach out to people and resources around you as you navigate the challenges of your own life.

Consider this: Usually when someone asks us for help, we're happy to provide it, delighted for the opportunity to feel competent and useful. So asking for help creates a win-win! Also, keep in mind that by reaching out for help, you're setting a great example for your children and the other adults in your life.

> ## *Reprise: You Can Learn How To Parent Yourself*

Gwen: Sometimes even as adults we still need parenting—and that includes parenting ourselves. When Seymour was dying and I wondered what would happen next, I comforted myself, just as I'd done when I was a child. Memories of being alone in the dark house during World War II came flooding back. I reminded myself that it was all going to be okay. Everything would work out. It's fascinating that those self-taught comforts from way-back-when were still useful to me decades later.

#15: Don't make promises you can't keep

Gwen: As I often say, I've eaten a steady diet of my own words for most of my life. There are many examples of this, but perhaps the most significant is when I declared, "I'll never get married again!" Seymour died when I was forty-two years old, and after a time I realized that if I continued doing what I was doing—running my household and finishing raising my children—I would most likely get married again. But I yearned to be on my own—after all, it would be the first time in so many years that I would be responsible only for myself. So I made this sweeping statement. And I made it often.

At the time, I truly meant what I said. I didn't want my freedom curtailed or my power taken away from me. I'd just been through the death of my husband and couldn't imagine having to endure that heartbreak again. In the end, just four years after my first husband died, something unexpected happened—I fell in love! George and I had this great romance, which was unplanned and had nothing to do with marriage. At the time I met him, finding a man was the furthest thing from my mind. But there you go—I ended up eating my words.

Instead of being stubborn and stopping myself from getting remarried simply because I had said I wouldn't, I chose to move into a new phase of happiness in my life. I learned to accept that things in the past were different, and I now had a new view. It's important not to beat yourself up about changing your mind based on your current reality.

The point is to not make exaggerated statements about things you can't predict. Comments like *I'll never talk to you again* or *I'll never move out of this town* are only valid in the moment. They are really ultimatums. You can't make predictions about how you'll be in the future since you haven't been there yet.

Amy: When I first moved to Boston with my best friend from college, Posy, I had no idea what I would do for work or a career. We knew no one but each other and set out on this big adventure together. I started my job at the advertising agency, and I dated a bit. Posy and I were out one night at a bar called Houlihan's, and I met a guy I really liked. I hadn't had many serious boyfriends previously, and after a while I even envisioned a future with this young man, who I'll call Paul. He met my family, and I met his. However, we didn't see each other often, and rarely on weekends because he was busy with work commitments and training for a marathon.

One night Posy and I ran into Paul's roommate. He confided in me that Paul was cheating on me with an old girlfriend. That was a punch in the gut. I was beyond crushed and heartbroken. I confronted Paul and broke up with him. I then proclaimed, "I'll never date a guy I meet in a bar ever again. You just can't trust them." Keep in mind that at the time, there was no online dating. Our only options were to meet someone at work or at a bar, or to be set up on a blind date!

It turns out that I did meet the next guy I dated at a bar—so much for my promise never to do that again. On our first date, I was almost two hours late because I was delayed at a client meeting. Without cell phones, there was no way to alert him. But, steadfast to the core, he waited for me right where he said he would be. Dependability was one of the things that really mattered to me at the time. Not only did I end up dating him, but I also married him!

It's easy to make these sweeping statements, but that's all they are—just words. Try to realize that you can't know your future, and when you proclaim "allness" statements—declarations about how something will be for *all time*—you may be creating false limitations for yourself. If you've already made similar statements, be willing to revisit your beliefs and update your thinking down the road. Reality only consists of what we know at the time.

We say things when we're sad or hurt in an attempt to protect ourselves in the future. When we say, *I'll never do this again!* we mean *I'll never let myself get hurt again.* It's understandable and okay to make these kinds of proclamations, but be open to revisiting them. When new circumstances or feelings present themselves, be willing to feast on your own words.

CHAPTER 9

The Master of Invention

"At this point, Bill, Amy, and I were all in school. Between the coursework and required internships, my master's program was very demanding. During my second year, I was placed at Family Service Association of Nassau County for an internship. Imagine a forty-four-year-old intern! As part of my work there, I organized a widows' group. It was successful, which was no surprise—after all, I'd been a widow for more than two years. While the others in the group were newly bereaved, I was a relative expert.

For my program development class, we were required to write a paper outlining a unique counseling program—something that didn't already exist. Off the top of my head, I wrote a plan for a bereavement center that would offer *support for widows, grieving parents, and siblings through individual, family, and group services. When my professor handed the graded paper back to me, he said it was a great idea and urged me to share it with my supervisor at Family Service. So I slipped the paper under Dr. Ambrosino's door. I was just finishing up my internship and preparing to graduate.*

That very night, Dr. A. called me and said he loved my idea and wanted to move ahead with it. He planned to create the bereavement center I had devised! On top of that, he offered me the position of director. He did warn me that he couldn't yet pay me since this was a new program and there wouldn't be any money coming in. Still, I accepted the job because I knew I'd gain valuable experience.

I couldn't believe my luck. Not one day out of social work school, and I was offered a directorship! Once again a job had been dropped in my lap. How's that for a new forty-four-year-old graduate?

I had no idea how to actually create this bereavement center. After all, I'd been told to come up with something new. This hadn't been done before, so there were no courses on the subject or manuals to follow. Of course there was bereavement—people died, and their loved ones grieved—but there was no working program to support people following a death. But with my two years of experience, I figured I knew as much as anyone, so I jumped right in.

At first it was slow going—after all, no one had really

heard about the center. Then, Dr. A. told me that the program had been offered a one-minute promotional commercial from a large New York TV outlet. It was slated to run in the middle of the night, but we accepted it anyway. I wrote the segment, then went into New York City to record it. For days, then weeks, after the spot aired, I was flooded with calls. But when I thought about it, this made complete sense. After all, who's awake in the wee hours of the morning? People who are grieving!

The center became a thriving entity almost overnight. We were so overwhelmed by clients that soon I had to hire help. I took on interns from other social work schools, did TV interviews, and gave lectures all over Nassau County. On top of that, I was finally receiving a paycheck. Setting out, I wasn't an experienced social worker, but I had all the expertise I needed to take that first step. The rest I learned on the job, eventually becoming a true expert in grief.

While I worked to manage this major shift in my life, I was also managing life as a single mom. My children were grown, yet I never stopped learning how to become a better parent. Case in point: When Amy came home from college, she wanted to see her friends, stay out late, and do whatever she wanted, but those weren't the rules of the house before she'd left. I realized that it was important to allow her the independence she was used to when living away. Now that she'd been on her own, with no one telling her what to do, I could no longer make rules for her behavior during her visits. And she was about to go even farther from home and experience even more independence!

By 1980, Bill had graduated from college, Amy was headed to a semester in London, and I had decided to leave the center to go into private practice. I created a home office, where I saw clients and held groups. I finally agreed to marry George, who had been patiently driving me to all those TV interviews and other events. Over time, he simply became part of my new life.

At forty-six years old, I had the exciting challenge of a new marriage and a flourishing career. I was also offered a position as an associate professor at Hofstra University (my alma mater). Soon I was teaching two classes there in addition to running my bereavement practice.

I wasn't the only one who achieved success during that time. By age twenty-two, Amy had finished college and was working in her first job, at an advertising agency. Eventually, she decided that she wanted to leave the agency to open a cake bakery. To me it was a shame because she had worked so hard to advance. On top of that, she had no business or bakery experience. I was surprised and concerned that Amy was not equipped to succeed in an endeavor as challenging as this one."

♪ LESSONS LEARNED ♪

> *#16: When the student is ready, the teacher appears*

Gwen: Previously I told the story about how I'd planned to get my PhD, but when the doctor suggested I spend more time with my son to help his stuttering, I put those plans on hold. I'll be honest—that was a major disappointment for me. And yet it was the right thing for me to do at the time. I couldn't possibly have known that life had something else in store in the form of getting my master's and starting the bereavement center. But it happened then because the timing was right!

Once the center was up and running, I was leading bereavement groups throughout the week. Over time, my program garnered profits and praise. I never would have been able to accomplish any of this had I not been ready, and had my "teacher," Sal Ambrosino, not appeared.

Crisis is stressful, yet often it's what opens people up to novel opportunities. If you can be open to receiving something new, the person you need to help you will appear.

After Seymour died, I was ready for that something new. I didn't know anything about social work, but when the opportunity to go to school arose, I took it. Try to embrace the different—the new and the challenging—and you'll find that you will be able to do amazing things. You simply need to believe in yourself, and when opportunities arise, realize that they are there for a reason.

Widowhood was a tremendous challenge, but it became a springboard into a whole new world. I was able to turn my grief into a teaching experience to help others. I realize now that everything I knew, I learned from working with my clients. They taught me so much about bereavement and grief. There was no written subject matter available at the time because it was a brand-new topic open for discussion.

You can see crisis as an opportunity for growth, or see it as "the end." After everything I'd been through, I knew how to take a life-altering tragedy and make it into something good. That's resilience.

It's like I always tell my clients: Try to learn from your bad experiences, even if it doesn't come naturally. You can often find that good can come from bad if you view it that way.

Amy: In 2020 when I started my very first virtual coaching group, Drive Your Life, I invited a woman who was an online acquaintance to join the group. Rosie was a happiness coach by profession. I asked if she would "audit" the group and participate but also give me some feedback at the end. It was a brand-new program I had developed to give women the tactics and strategies they would need to take action in their lives.

As part of the process, the women chose one area that they wanted either to improve or to explore. Rosie chose building and growing her coaching practice. Her goal was to decide what direction she should take and what services she would offer. It turned out, in fact, that as she went through the Drive Your Life process, she realized that she actually might be interested in a job placement. She hadn't really considered the idea of working for someone before. And during that eight-week span, a job opportunity surprisingly came across her path. She ended up being hired at a mental health day program for adults, and she loved it.

In her feedback on my program, she shared that she had learned more about herself and become open to the possibility that her concrete plan could be something different from what she had envisioned.

When she allowed herself to be led toward a different path, she followed it! She was ready for a change, though she didn't know it, and the vehicle for that change appeared.

There can be a ripeness to take that next step. As we learn more about ourselves, the path will open up. I love the line in the musical *Into the Woods* when Cinderella says, "Opportunity is not a lengthy visitor." Opportunities can be fleeting, so we need to stay alert to spot them when they appear.

What is in front of you that you can lean into? What can you see as an opportunity? You may have to try harder at first to see the options, and you may have to give yourself a little push forward, but I have found that any action almost always feels better than standing still.

#17: You can't put the toothpaste back in the tube

Gwen: We've all had that moment when we squeeze out more toothpaste than we need, but we know we cannot get the excess back in the tube. The same goes for our life experiences. Once you've experienced new things and learned new behaviors that are positive or that give you pleasure, you don't want to go back to the previous ones. Old behaviors can be limiting and in comparison to new ones, may not be attractive anymore.

You can't unlearn what you've learned or unsee what you've seen. You can't erase what you now know, and that's okay—it's part of growing.

When your kids go away to college and they're living on their own, it can be difficult for both of you when they come back home for vacation. They've lived independently without your constant influence, and you can't undo the independence they've gained. This was illustrated to me when Amy came home from college and wanted to relinquish the old house rules we'd had in place. It was a tremendous opportunity to turn the situation into an emancipation experience for both of us.

Sometimes we turn into helicopter parents

when our children return home. We monitor them and do too much for them as a way to keep them infantilized. We want to prove our value as parents. Yet you can't reverse your children's life experiences and return them to their dependent state. You can't unring the bell.

Once I realized that there was no going back with Amy, I grew to welcome the change. It was a chance to get to know Amy as the new adult she had become.

Amy: During Covid, many people were given the opportunity to work from home. They got used to the ease of not having to get dressed up for work or commute to their offices. It was the first time in our history that so much work could be done completely from home. It came about abruptly, yet it couldn't be undone. Now that many are back to work in a more conventional sense, even part time, I hear people—mainly in the younger generation—complaining about having to go into an office. I find that somewhat amusing, as for me, until recently, work was always going to a place of business. People now miss the ability to do laundry and start dinner during their workday as they did during Covid. They liked not having to fuss with business clothes. Mainly I believe they enjoyed the flexibility that working from home afforded them. And most likely it felt less stressful. We can't reverse the experience they had, or erase it from their minds. It just represents a new challenge.

It's important to remember that while looking back can be appealing, it can also be a trap. If you don't have the ability to change your current circumstances, you have to accept what is. When it comes to going back to the office, for example, we simply have to accept it if that's what is required.

Part of the challenge is that we often fear change, without considering its potential benefits. We can focus on the positives—like having more interaction with coworkers or being guided in person by our mentors—as a way to accept the change.

Either way, sometimes a situation just is what it is. You can't put the toothpaste back in the tube!

> **#18: You can tell your adult children what to do, but only tell them once**

Gwen: Shortly after Amy told me about her plan to open a bakery, I called her and suggested that she connect with a friend's daughter who was in business school and could help her create a business plan. Amy, however, said she didn't need or want that help. A week later I called her again. This time I suggested that she should perhaps work in a bakery before opening one herself. Again, Amy dismissed the idea. So I offered her my support and waited to see if she would make good on her plan. And she did, opening a successful bakery. It wasn't easy, but she did it.

Amy rejected my suggestions twice. Eventually, I learned to keep my thoughts to myself. I consider this a classic example of this lesson, and fortunately it's one that has a happy ending. It was difficult to keep my thoughts to myself, but I knew that voicing my doubt over and over again would not be helpful to Amy and would most likely fracture our close relationship.

Amy intuitively knew what she wanted, and she didn't want advice from other people. And if I may say, she did an amazing job! She was right. She needed to do this on her own, her way. Parents have to take their hands off everything their children do. They have to separate themselves and know that their child will learn on their own. Experience is a great teacher.

I realized that my role was changing from mother to mentor. Amy saw that I had actual knowledge worth sharing, but my help was only welcome when she asked for it. This can be a difficult transition for some parents to make and accept, but it's important.

If they don't hear it the FIRST time, they are not going to hear it later on.

Amy: You can look at this from two perspectives: from the child's or the adult's. I love this lesson as an adult child. Who wants their parents telling them what to do over and over again? However, as the parent of adult children, I find this rule very challenging to follow! My children would probably agree. I like to give my opinion, possibly too much, and it's not unusual for me to repeat my suggestions. This is one of the reasons I decided to write this book. I wanted to share some of my mother's wisdom so others could benefit from it.

My younger daughter is admittedly a bit messy (as I can be), and when she was growing up, her room was always cluttered with an array of things strewn on the bed, on the floor, on chairs, etc. My husband and I would frequently tell her to clean her room. We said it over and over again. It was a common refrain in our home. Jessie recently told me that it wasn't until she grew up and had her own apartment that keeping her space neat was important to her. Now that it is, she doesn't need to be told.

I know my adult children are competent at running their own lives. But it's difficult for me, and I would guess many others, to turn off "parenting mode." Still, we need to trust our children to make their own decisions. Go ahead and offer that advice once, but if they don't hear it then, they won't hear it the tenth time, either!

Another aspect that I think is important to recognize here is that when we keep offering our unsolicited advice over and over again, it's because we're convinced of our own rightness. The truth is, our way might not be *the* only way, or even the best way. In exploring their own path, your children could actually discover a better way, or at least a way that works better for them.

CHAPTER 10

Life Support

"Time went on. Then the world took a turn. On a visit to Amy's house, we witnessed two planes crashing into the World Trade Center. It was a horror that no one could have predicted, and we were thrust into a national crisis. Almost three thousand people were killed in nearby New York City.

Fate placed me in the position to help during a national catastrophe—September 11 created a living laboratory for grief. Widows, children, siblings, and parents flooded into my office day and night for weeks, months, and even years. I was practically on retainer to the NYFD.

At some moments I feared that I would drown in all their tears. To manage it all, I decided to focus on each person, one at a time. Instead of seeing the entire crowd or the collective *tragedy they had experienced, I looked at each individual, and each experience, on their own. Fortunately, it worked. I quickly learned to interact with each person as if he or she was the only client I had. That helped me move forward and continue to help, despite the scope of what we were all dealing with.*

I know for many people, life starts to settle down in their sixties and seventies, but for me these were highly productive years! At seventy, when most people are retiring, my career was accelerating. September 11 was a historic catastrophe, and I found myself more enmeshed in work than I had ever been in my life. I was working full time, and my bereavement center experience brought requests for lectures, training in local schools, and consultations.

How lucky can you get? All my life I had been the youngest person to accomplish things, as both a high school graduate and graduate school graduate. Now I was the oldest!"

LESSONS LEARNED

> *#19: Don't ask "why" questions*

Gwen: When disaster happens, whether personal or universal, people often ask, *What did I do to deserve this?* We equate disaster with our own behavior, thinking it was caused by us. After the 9/11 catastrophe, my private practice was flooded with one beautiful young widow after another. I was confronted with hundreds of people asking the same question: *Why did this happen to me, to my family, and to my children? We are good people and we lead good lives.*

In reality, tragedy has nothing to do with your behavior. The catastrophe occurred outside your experience. Life isn't about getting what you do or don't deserve. We tend to personalize everything and make it about us, but it's not.

I understood this tendency to ask why because I did it myself. When my forty-nine-year-old husband was diagnosed with an inoperable brain tumor, I, too, asked why it happened. I contacted doctors and scientists all over the country, asking each of them,

"Why did my husband get a brain tumor? Where did it come from?" I needed an answer, but I never found it. Everyone I reached out to said the same thing: "I don't know." It was through this experience that I learned this life lesson. The fact is that there is never one simple answer for what transpires in life.

When we try to deal with what has happened, we often put ourselves in the center of it, making it all about us. That's the wrong place to be. All you can deal with is what is in front of you. Focus on that, instead of trying to figure out how or why it got there.

For each widow I saw, her personal loss was the biggest loss she could imagine, because in her world it was the greatest loss she had ever experienced. It may have felt like she was the only one, but she wasn't, just as I wasn't.

During that national tragedy, I realized that what had happened to us individually with Seymour's death had now happened to thousands of people. My personal catastrophe brought me the experience I needed to deal with what was now a public catastrophe. It had become magnified beyond what I could have ever imagined. If there was a "why" in his death, perhaps that's part of it, but I'll never truly know.

When we ask why, we're looking for a simple answer to a complicated question, and we'll probably never find it—at least, not one that satisfies us. When you find yourself asking why, try to remember that while it's natural to ask that question, it's futile.

The best, and really the only, way to deal with tragedy or catastrophe is not to ask why but rather to ask, *How am I going to deal with this?* Spend your time and energy focusing on that.

Amy: It's natural to want to know why things happen. As a young teenager I wondered why my father had to die. I had so little life experience at the time, and I didn't understand why my world had to change so drastically.

If we can move past our desire to know why, we can focus on the "how"—how to stop ruminating, and how to put our energies into dealing with what's happened. In my work, I focus on *how* to take action and move forward. Just like my mother ended up counseling people who were grieving, maybe that's why I ended up focusing on ways to move forward and gain a sense of control.

My daughter Jessie always did well at school and received good grades. That is, until the summer leading into her sophomore year of high school, when she complained constantly about the assigned reading for her AP English class. I thought it was just a case of not wanting to do schoolwork during vacation time. The same occurred the following summer with her required reading. Again, I dismissed it as teenage complaining.

But then, when Jessie took the pre-ACT test, her score was almost the lowest possible. It was so shocking given what her academic grades were that I felt something was wrong. I decided to have her go through neuropsychological testing to ascertain whether she had any kind of learning disability. It seemed very late in the game, but my gut was telling me to pursue this possibility.

When my husband and I went in to receive the results, we were stunned by what we learned. They told us that Jessie had dyslexia, along with a processing issue. We also found out that testing for dyslexia should be done around age six, and in order to be effective, dyslexia interventions need to occur early in elementary school. We were well beyond that.

Of course I asked why. Why did this happen to Jessie? It seemed so unfair. I also couldn't understand how she had gotten through all those years of schooling doing so well with this major learning disability. I felt that I had let her down as a parent and wondered why neither we nor her teachers caught this. (The answer the psychologists gave was that she was smart enough to guess her way through the academics up until that point.)

Then my action-oriented instincts kicked in. I decided that I wasn't going to let this very late diagnosis have any more of an ill effect on Jessie, or her confidence, than it already had. When I spoke to her high school, they were neither sympathetic nor helpful. They said she was doing fine and didn't need help or accommodations. I then found an education advocate and went to work. We set up meetings, I found a reading tutor for Jessie, and I learned how to get accommodations for the SAT and ACT. Unfortunately the ACT wouldn't grant the accommodation. Jessie had taken the SAT countless times and even with tutoring couldn't bring up her score.

So I went back again and appealed the ACT's decision. At the very last minute, Jessie was granted the accommodation she deserved, and she took the test one more time. Her score finally matched her academic ability, and she got into several of the more challenging colleges she had applied to. Jessie went from frustrated and ready to throw in the towel to feeling confident about what she'd accomplished.

Jessie has now dedicated her career to working

in accessibility with those who have disabilities. This is a bonus that came from her diagnosis. She found a passion and a career that were born from one of her greatest challenges—yet another silver lining.

Through it all we both learned that you can ask why, but soon after, you have to decide what you can do to actually change the situation.

> ## Reprise: We Often Worry About The Wrong Things

Gwen: I worked with a lot of 9/11 firefighters' widows in my bereavement practice. I used to routinely ask them, "Did you worry about your husband's work? Did you worry about him walking into flaming buildings?" And although it was not what anyone would call a "safe" job, not one of them ever said they worried about their husband dying at work. They said the men were well trained and well prepared. They were doing work they loved, and they never worried.

On that September morning, these women all said, *I'll see you later* to their husbands as they left for work. Who expected a plane to fly into a building causing them to rush into a fire-filled skyscraper? Who would have thought of that? No one. Whatever they did worry about turned out to be the wrong thing.

People whose lives are always in danger don't worry because they are confident they know what they're doing. It's the unexpected events that they aren't equipped to deal with.

> #20: *The best way to get through loss is to make friends with the pain*

Gwen: The wives, children, parents, and friends of those who died on 9/11 faced a depth of pain that seemed impossible to survive. In our sessions, I counseled the widows not to fight that pain, but to accept it as the cost of loving. I told them to understand that the pain was going to be their companion. They needed to learn to walk next to it for years to come as they learned to rebuild their lives.

The learning curve was steep. In one day their whole lives changed. Sudden, unexpected death brings a unique perspective that's different from protracted illness or a death that's otherwise anticipated. There was no preparation for this.

There are other kinds of pain we must also learn to befriend. The loss of a spouse through divorce can create a pain similar to death, when the divorce is not your choice. It's the death of your marriage, and so the pain of loss can be similar. For many women, divorce alters their status in the world. It can be an embarrassment or create an unwanted change in their relationship to their children and their friends.

Divorced women receive no casseroles—no tea and no sympathy.

Then, there are people living with chronic physical pain. They have to live their lives right alongside that pain. My lifelong friend Sylvia Brown was stricken with debilitating arthritis at a relatively young age. She needed two canes to walk, yet she never ceased to amaze me with her stoic, can-do attitude. When I asked her how she got through each day and every physical challenge, she told me that she wanted to live her life. If she didn't force herself to get up each morning and accept the pain, she would be in bed all day. Sylvia had learned to make friends with her pain. It was her only choice.

Amy: I had a client, Laura, who decided to make some changes to her home. She wanted to clean out her basement and use it as a playroom for her grandchildren. Initially, I thought what she needed was an action plan and the accountability to help her get the job done.

As we worked through the steps, Laura realized that something was holding her back. During the process, she shared that it was painful for her to remove all the things that were stored in her basement and to part with those items because when she was a child they had a house fire. Her family lost much of their belongings. So that experience stayed with her, and try as she might, she couldn't let go of that pain.

Over time Laura learned tactics and strategies to help her move through the struggle of having to sort through and part with some of her things. Saving possessions in her basement wouldn't protect her from the potential for future loss. As my mother would say, that's just magical thinking. It helped her to admit that the childhood pain of loss would always be with her, but she could overcome it to create something meaningful for herself. She could make friends with the pain.

As someone who is focused on action and "doing," I find it difficult to sit back and accept circumstances. It's important to humble yourself with the fact that there are things you can't change or control. I know that when Laura brought her grandchildren down to that playroom, she often thought of her own childhood and what she lost in the fire. Keeping those memories close also allowed her to take pride in her ability to move past her feelings and clear out her basement.

Can you use the pain in your life, whether psychological or physical, to help you move forward?

Can you see that it can make you stronger or more resilient? And if you can't, can you accept that it is there now, and will continue to be there, as part of you? Sometimes if you really look back, you can see how past hurts can help you and even set you up for future successes.

Reprise: There Are No Bad Experiences In Life, Just The Ones You Don't Learn From

Gwen: Some of the 9/11 widows saw their new circumstance as an opportunity—though an unwelcome one—to create change in their lives. As a result, they went to new places and had new experiences. One of the widows I worked with went on to become a state legislator. Prior to 9/11 she had been a telephone worker, with no college education. The crisis gave some people an opportunity for growth, but others saw it as nothing but loss and an ending.

For my part, I had meaningful rehearsals for my 9/11 experience as a widow, then as a grief counselor. Growing up during World War II, with all the challenges that entailed, equipped me to live through these long nights of worrying. When Seymour was diagnosed with a brain tumor, I stayed awake wondering what would happen when he died and I had to keep my children and my family going. But this wasn't new territory for me. It was hard, and I was scared, but I knew I could get through it, as I'd gotten through the challenges I'd faced as a child.

When I became a widow myself, although it was a tragic experience, it helped me learn how to deal with grief and loss. Then, when 9/11 happened, I was ready and able to help those hundreds of widows who needed me. September 11 was my learning laboratory—learning to live with another kind of loss.

People are still dealing with 9/11. After all, you don't process grief overnight. Like learning to befriend the pain, to some extent the grief is always with you. But in addition to being a friend, it can also be a great teacher. And it may be that the experiences you're grappling with today will enable you to deal with challenges that will arise in the future—or help others to do so . . . as long as you make the effort to learn from your experiences.

CHAPTER 11

New Roles to Play

"Long before 9/11, back in 1987, Amy married a wonderful man—Bob—and in 1992 they welcomed a beautiful baby girl, Samantha. At age sixty-one, I became a grandmother. I was still living in New York, so this brought yet another new adventure: becoming a visiting grandmother. When Amy brought Samantha into our world, the big challenge became how to overcome distance with love.

I was working full time, traveling frequently, and Burlington was more than four hours from Massapequa. But I decided that distance would not defeat the grandmother in me. Have car, will travel! The bonding experience that started with Samantha grew along with Amy's family—soon Jimmy and then Jessie were added!

Jumping hurdles instead of being stymied is my way. With careful planning and a strong determination, I (and often George) learned to bond long-distance. Over the next twenty-five years, I made sure to never miss a birthday, holiday, recital, theater performance, ball game, or vacation. Neither rain nor snow . . . We showed up and participated as though we lived around the corner. Regardless of the distance, I bonded with those grandchildren tightly and forever. I went from parent to Nana in what seemed like a short period of time.

Now, as I reflect on the years when my parents were grandparents, I realize that they did not prioritize getting to know and spend time with my children. But I made the decision to do the opposite."

LESSONS LEARNED

> *#21: Your children were not put on this earth to make you happy*

Gwen: I think the expectation of most parents is *My children are going to make me very happy. They're going to make me very proud. They will be accomplished and smart, and everyone is going to say, "You're just like your mother!" or "You're just like your father!"*

The reality is that many adult children say, *I'm not like my mother or my father. And as a matter of fact, I've been spending my whole life trying to be as different from them as I can!*

The lesson here for parents is to shift your expectations that your children were put on this earth to make you feel good about yourself. They are not here to achieve what you were not able to achieve. You don't want to expect your child to live out your own unrealized dreams.

The sign of successful parenting isn't that your children are just like you; it's that you are no longer needed. You teach your child to use a cup so you don't have to feed them. You teach them how to get dressed so they can do it for themselves. As they grow older, your children shouldn't need your advice and your approval. Successful separation is the sign of good parenting. Remember that!

Parents can find this rule especially challenging when their children choose a lifestyle that is different from their own. It's important to realize their purpose here is not to please you. Remind yourself that they are individuals with their own choices and their own paths. If you've been a successful parent, you can watch your children walk on their own and lead their own lives. You can also have a life that's independent of them.

Young children say, *My mother says, my father says.* As they grow older they say, *My teacher says, my friend says.* Final growth is reached when they say, *This is what I think.* That autonomy is a true sign of independence and adulthood.

Amy: This is another interesting lesson to consider as both a child and a parent. We want the freedom as the child, but we may not want to give it as the parent.

From the minute you watch your baby crawl

away from you and cheer them on, you're giving them encouragement to leave you. We don't think of it that way when it's happening.

When I graduated from college, I planned to move to Boston. New York City felt too overwhelming, and Boston seemed like the next logical location to start my life. My mother encouraged me in this direction, and frankly I don't think my decision affected her at all. She was used to not living anywhere near her own parents or having them as part of her day-to-day life. She had just gotten remarried and was in the throes of that romance, plus she was busy growing and developing the bereavement center.

As my children graduated from college, I have to admit that I wanted them to settle close to Bob and me. I don't feel guilty for that because if you love your children and enjoy being with them, it's natural to want them near you. But I accepted that they needed to make their own decisions.

I work with a lot of empty nesters, and this lesson is one of the most difficult to accept. Separation is painful. It's viewed as a loss when you are no longer the influential parent of your child. As mothers we pour so much of ourselves into our children from the time we are pregnant and ever after. Their lives are intertwined with ours, and we have the ability to steer them by making choices that parents make. When they grow up and are able to make their own decisions, we can find ourselves out of a job and without the influence we've had for so long.

When women I work with express conflict with their children, the overriding challenge is often that their offspring are not doing what they want them to do. What can be tricky is that we want our children to be happy, yet what makes them happy is not always what makes us happy.

If you're a parent, do you find yourself steering your children in the direction that you want them to go or that benefits you? Think about this lesson and whether you realize that your adult children are free to make their own choices regardless of your wishes.

You don't have to like it, but you probably need to accept it.

This can be one of the greatest challenges of parenting our children when they reach adulthood, and eventually when they have families of their own.

#22: You can learn from your past

Gwen: We should never underestimate the power of *negative modeling*. The way I was raised prompted me to decide that I would never raise a child in the same way. My mother had me, then left me alone or with others much of the time. She paid little to no attention to me, putting her needs above my own. She and my father, who loved to move around a lot, gave no thought to how that would affect their growing children. When I was twenty-one, they moved to Florida, leaving me in a house by myself.

My parents were at my home when I was about to give birth to Amy. When I went into labor, my husband was on a worksite and unreachable, so my parents drove me to the hospital. They dropped me off at the parking lot by myself. My mother said, "I want to go shopping." There I was, abandoned again. All I knew was that, however I had been raised, I was not going to repeat that pattern with my own children.

Not surprisingly, my parents were also absentee grandparents. Periodically, they would appear from their travels, and it was always a short and quarrelsome visit. My children never really got to know them, and I often thought, *They'd be better off without those grandparents.*

I decided that when I became a grandmother, this would be the model for what I would *not* do. Fortunately, negative modeling had a positive effect!

Ask yourself what you would have wanted your parents to do differently, and then do that . . . You can choose how you want to parent. You can revise your past by turning negative modeling into positive behavior on your own part.

Most people say, *This is what I learned at home* . . . But remember, there are other voices besides those of your parents. Sometimes our parents are not our best teachers—especially when they're teaching us behaviors we don't want to emulate. But that's okay—there are many other teachers and fill-in parents in life.

Amy: At the time that my father was diagnosed and then dying, I gained a lot of weight. I was a sophomore in high school, and looking back, I guess I was "eating my feelings." I didn't understand it then, but somehow overeating provided some kind of comfort for me. Before I knew it, I was significantly overweight, and that of course brought on a lot of its own challenges for a girl my age during the high school years. Over time I also learned that putting on extra weight can provide a metaphorical buffer that protects one from outside hurt.

It was very painful and difficult to suddenly be an overweight teenager during high school and then college. Although I lost the majority of the weight I'd gained during the end of college and shortly thereafter, I always struggled with my weight. I was constantly trying to lose weight or simply maintain it. Those early challenges really stayed with me.

After selling The Icing on the Cake in 1993, I was a stay-at-home mom until my youngest, Jessie, was in middle school. At the time, my son, Jimmy, was in high school and Samantha was in college.

I tried yet another in a long line of weight loss plans. I found that it worked well for both my husband and me. I decided then that I wanted to help others with their weight loss challenges as well. I became a health coach for the program Bob and I had used, and I worked with people (mainly women) to learn the habits of health and follow the program that I had found success with.

Ultimately I worked as a health coach for seven years and supported hundreds of clients virtually and in person. I share this here as an example of how you can learn from your past. You can take personal challenges and turn them into positives. My mother's example of turning widowhood into social work followed this same principle. I urge you to look back at what you see as the difficulties and challenges that life has thrown your way. It's often easiest to squash them down and forget about them. But if they surface, think about how you can take the bad and make it into something good. Turn them into a fertile field for growth and development.

Take my mother, for example—she came home after school to an empty house, with a key around her neck. But she made sure that I would come home to a loving mother with open arms.

CHAPTER 12

Lucky Accident

"I started smoking cigarettes when I was sixteen. Like most addicts, I stopped and started during the many years and decades that followed. Most of the time, I snuck around and lied about the habit. When I attended conferences, I hid outside the buildings with the other addicts in what we called the Leper Colony. The addiction was so powerful that in order to keep smoking, I became a consummate liar and an absolute fraud. I pretended that I had stopped smoking, and to support this lie I presented two personas. The public persona did not smoke, but the private persona did. This continued on and off for years. I think of myself as someone who is able to do anything, yet I was defeated by my addiction.

When I was eighty-six, I was outside my house after dinner doing my typical sneak. It was a dark night and I tripped, fell, and broke four ribs. I went to the emergency room, and a routine x-ray revealed a mass in my right lung. I thought that my luck had run out. Subsequently, one third of my lung was removed. The test results showed small-cell lung cancer, which is normally a speedy killer. Yet my incredible luck held out—the tumor was encapsulated and had not spread. My surgeon told me that this was nothing short of a miracle because for this type of cancer, once the symptoms appear, it's almost always too late.

I had dodged a bullet, but I realized that nothing improves with age. George was ninety, and I was eighty-six—we were never going to be healthier than we were then. Other health issues might soon arise, and I didn't want Amy and Bill to have to come and care for me as they'd done with my cancer. I decided to move to Massachusetts to be closer to my children.

Yet while the decision was clear to me, George was of another opinion. We debated on and off for weeks without any meeting of the minds. In the end, I knew I was right, and I refused to stay in New York. So George, in the name of marital harmony, agreed to the move. One of us was happy with the decision, and the other went kicking and screaming, but we entered our new life together. I can't blame George because he'd lived in the New York area most of his life, and he was very much a creature of habit. But it was the right thing to do. Plus, I'd already learned my lesson about life: In the end, everything would turn out to be good.

I embraced turning ninety! Another decade and another new kind of life, full of challenges and unique experiences, was at my doorstep. We moved into a beautiful apartment with all the services we needed, and we were just five minutes away from Amy and Bob. We dusted off our bridge skills and began to make new friends.

Then, we faced another historic situation. The Covid-19 pandemic struck, and given our ages we were identified as being at very high risk. By this time, I was ninety and George was ninety-four. Suddenly we were being treated as though we were an endangered species, with restrictions placed on us and our social activities.

I wasn't having it. I decided that we were too old to die young, and declared my own war on Covid. Having been born during the polio epidemic and been witness to other international tragedies, I saw Covid, by comparison, as much ado about nothing. To me, it seemed that the cure, or in this case the efforts at prevention, were worse than the disease! So I ignored the rules concerning isolation. I found kindred spirits from the bridge group, and although the senior center was closed down, we continued to play at our apartment. I served tea in china cups, no one wore a mask, and all of us sailed through the pandemic without ever contracting Covid.

How lucky can you get? To be born during one epidemic

and face old age in another, and survive both! So there we were, passing our physicals each time. Every day I walked for one to two miles. Sure, we lived the life of the elderly, but we were also fit! Still, George disliked our new community and longed for the "old country," although no one we knew there was still alive. Our friends were dying, and we were among the last survivors of our cohort.

And that's where I am today—living, thriving, and always and forever still learning. I look forward to what adventures are yet to be!"

LESSONS LEARNED

> *#23: Don't make it bigger than it has to be*

Gwen: At eighty-six, I was faced with what for many people is the deadliest thing that could happen—a diagnosis of lung cancer. I cheered myself by saying at least I knew how I got it! Fortunately, I found a wonderful thoracic surgeon, who cautioned that the mass needed to be attended to immediately. George and I were going to California for his ninetieth birthday, but we knew we had to change our plans.

Someone else would have said, *I'm going to die from this*, but I didn't think that way. I felt grateful that, thanks ironically to my smoking habit and those broken ribs, we discovered the mass. I had the surgery, lost one-third of my lung, and took it in stride.

So often when we receive difficult news, we go to the worst-case scenario. We think our life is over—figuratively or quite literally. But I didn't. I vowed that I would not make the situation bigger than it had to be, and we'd simply take it one step at a time.

Then, after we moved to Massachusetts, George and I made friends by playing bridge locally twice a week. That was, until Covid-19. We were told, *Don't eat out! Don't see people!* To me, that was just the mentality of waiting to die. So many older people were withering away in their homes and apartments while their well-meaning families left them alone. I was not going to curtail my life that way.

Amy didn't agree with me. She didn't want to visit us in case she was harboring the virus and might unknowingly pass it along. The only in-person contact she would allow was to have us over to sit on her outside deck.

Still, we persisted in inviting friends to the apartment to play bridge. I simply repeated my mantra from my nights alone during the World War II air raids: *Everything will be all right.*

Amy: I've been hearing this lesson since I was seven years old and in Miss Onderdonk's second-grade classroom. That teacher assigned more homework than should have been allowable by law. Every day I'd come home and sit on our porch and cry to my mother that I had too much homework. I was crying real tears. It all seemed so unfair and, quite frankly, almost insurmountable. My mom's reply was always *If you had started your homework instead of crying about it, you'd be done by now.* It was all about not making things bigger than they had to be. I can sometimes tend to over-focus on problems and sometimes blow them out of proportion. But remembering this lesson has helped me put situations into perspective, especially as an adult.

I think it's natural for things to escalate in our minds without our permission. Another approach you can take when something upsets or derails you is to ask yourself if this issue will be as important to you in one week, one month, or one year. It doesn't serve us to ruminate about things that may not even matter just a short distance down the road.

> *#24: You can't put your head on someone else's shoulders*

Gwen: After the lung cancer experience, I wanted to move closer to my children, but George didn't want to leave Massapequa. He hated change of any kind and simply didn't want to go. But I was adamant that my children's lives should not revolve around our health.

I presented many solid arguments for all the reasons why we should move. I was like a lawyer trying to sway a jury to my point of view.

In the end, I respected the fact that George and I were totally different people. The thought of moving to Massachusetts didn't disturb me or cause me any anxiety. Perhaps all that moving around I'd done as a child prepared me for this later move. George, on the other hand, had lived in his childhood home until he got married.

At first, I was irritated that George didn't see things my way, but then I realized, of course he doesn't. We're two different people. When it seems like things are escalating in your mind, it's not always about you. You need to understand that it can be about the other person, too. Stop to ask yourself:

What does this situation really mean to each of us?

Finally, I accepted that I couldn't pass my attitude, my love for my children, or my life experiences on to George, and I told him that he could stay in New York if he wanted to. He was never happy about moving, but he decided to do it anyway.

You have to learn to respect the differences.

Amy: This lesson has perhaps been the most valuable to me in my adult life. It's my nature to help others and often to give advice or coaching. This lesson reminds me that we can only have so much say in what other people do or don't do.

I worked virtually with a woman from Chicago, Carla, who had a challenging home life but didn't want to recognize it. She was warm and loving, but her husband didn't treat her well, and she accepted his verbal, and in some cases physical, abuse. It was difficult for her to share some of the circumstances because she felt she was betraying her husband in some way. She had also been raised to "stand by your man," and it was difficult for her to move past that.

While hoping to help her see how unhealthy her situation was, I tried to offer ways she could leave. But she was steadfast in her desire to keep her family together, even though her two sons were now grown. She'd gotten so used to this poor treatment that I think it seemed normal to her.

I felt frustrated and ineffective knowing how complacent Carla had become, but I couldn't transfer my own experiences and knowledge to her. It was difficult, but necessary, to admit that I just could not put my head on her shoulders.

This lesson can be useful within your family or work life as well. In the end, people only have their own history and experiences to go by when making decisions.

It's also useful to understand how easy it is for us, once again, to become convinced of our own rightness. We feel strongly because to us, all the pieces seem to fit together in only one way—the way we see it! But others are working with different pieces, and what's right for us genuinely may not be right for them. Sometimes people just need to do what they need to do, and that's part of their journey and their learning.

> *#25: Nothing improves with age, but maturity and experience can improve your attitude*

Gwen: We're often told that wisdom comes with age, but that's not a given. It's like the saying "Time heals all wounds." Well, no, it doesn't—at least, not on its own. It takes work. Similarly, getting old is not the same as taking all your experiences and incorporating them into the repertoire of your behaviors.

By now, you've read my favorite adage many times: *There are no bad experiences, only ones you don't learn from.* Well, that didn't come naturally to me. Situations don't transform magically before our eyes; we have to apply our attitude and insights to make them good. We have to actively seek the learning and continue to find the silver lining.

EPILOGUE

Gwen: As I reflect on the nine decades of my life, I go back to the question I asked at the beginning of this book: *How do you get to be the luckiest woman in the world?*

Until you have lived through real life experiences, there's no way to evaluate them. It's taken me more than ninety-three years of life to appreciate the true value of being on my own while knowing my family was supporting me. I see now that they stood in the background to watch me act out my life.

In writing this book, I realize that I had the right parents for me. Our first teachers are our parents, and my parents taught me how to be on my own early in my life. They used the show-and-tell method. I watched their behavior and that's how I learned. Minnie demonstrated her courage and bravery going outside the margins to use the Kenny method to help her child get through polio without braces.

How frightening it must have been to go against the medical advice of the day.

For his part, my father demonstrated bravery in his determination to get ahead in life. He moved his family to a new state during a world war. He demonstrated the courage of his own convictions and a belief in his own abilities.

It's true that my mother put me in the care of others and that my parents were mostly hands off, but that is what created the self-reliance and independence I've called on my whole life. It was the making of me and the foundation for the resiliency I would need later on.

Writing this book taught me that I had just the parents I needed, even if they weren't the ones I wanted or appreciated at the time. It didn't seem so then, but with the perspective of time, I can finally see it. I learned from every one of the challenges I faced in those early years.

As a result, I truly feel like the luckiest woman in the world.

Amy: Hopefully now you can see why I was compelled to write this book and share these lessons. My mother's wisdom has provided so much help and guidance for our family, along with hundreds of widows and their families. I hope that in her insights, you can find help and support for your own life's challenges.

ACKNOWLEDGMENTS

The definition of the word *acknowledgment* is recognition or favorable notice of an act or achievement. The people that I want to acknowledge for this book deserve far more than just a "favorable notice"!

Writing a book is far more challenging than I anticipated or even imagined. It's a labor of love that requires the author to live within the book for a long time. In the case of this book, I wanted to share the amazing story of my mother's life as well as the teachings she has imparted to me throughout my own life.

I thank my mother, Gwen Borden, for who she was before I was born and for the unique and incredible mother she has been to me my entire life.

My two daughters, Samantha and Jessie, supported me throughout this process and offered just the right amount of help and guidance I needed when I needed it.

My husband, Bob, has been a steady force throughout our marriage and during the creation of this book. He rode the roller coaster of ups and downs with me and deserves a lot of credit for helping me stay the course.

My editor, Kelly Madrone, has been nothing short of fantastic. Her generosity of time and spirit, her expertise, her patience, and her thoughtful suggestions have combined to make this book possible.

I am grateful to Girl Friday Productions for their guidance, knowledge, and patience throughout the publishing process.

Thank you also to my readers, Donna Gregorio, Cheryl Grasso, and Jodie Blase, for their willingness to preview the book in its original form and for their honest feedback. I'd like to give a special thanks to Donna as she has been with me from the start and has provided practical and caring advice and support all along the way.

I appreciate each and every person who spoke to me about this book and offered support and who will read and hopefully find value in the story and lessons it shares.

ABOUT THE AUTHORS

Photo © Mariah Gale

AMY GOOBER is an action and accountability coach dedicated to helping women reclaim their time, prioritize themselves, and take control of their lives. A dynamic speaker and workshop leader, Amy empowers women to focus on their goals and ensure they find a place for themselves on their own to-do lists.

She is the creator of Drive Your Life, a transformative group-coaching program designed to help women step into the driver's seat of their own lives with confidence and purpose. With a bachelor of science degree in psychology from Cornell University, Amy has leveraged her education and diverse experiences to support women through pivotal life transitions.

Amy's entrepreneurial journey began in 1986 when she founded The Icing on the Cake, a successful cake bakery in the Boston area, at just twenty-six years old. After building a thriving business, she passed it on to her employees so she could shift her focus to raising her three children. In 2013, Amy embraced a new path as a health coach, transforming the lives of more than seven hundred clients with her compassionate guidance.

At sixty, she launched her practice as an action coach, combining her professional and personal experiences to create a multifaceted business that includes group coaching, women's trips, and in-person events. She is also the founder of Better Together Events, which connects and inspires midlife women, and Wandering Women Travel, which offers women the chance to travel solo while enjoying the support and camaraderie of like-minded voyagers.

Inspired by the wisdom and life lessons of her ninety-three-year-old mother, Amy cowrote *My Mother Always Says* to share their combined reflections and practical advice for living with purpose, humor, and resilience.

Amy lives outside of Boston with her husband, Bob, and is the proud mother of three adult children. Her work continues to inspire women to embrace their own journeys and discover new possibilities at every stage of life.

ABOUT THE AUTHORS

GWEN BORDEN'S professional and personal journey is a testament to courage and compassion. A former teacher and social worker, Gwen designed and directed a bereavement center at Family & Childrens Association of Nassau County. This center was the first of its kind, supporting families through the challenges of death and dying.

Later, she worked as a bereavement specialist in private practice. Gwen counseled hundreds of widows and families during the harrowing aftermath of 9/11. She still supports some of these widows today, more than twenty years later.

Gwen holds degrees from Hofstra University, the University of Michigan, and the Adelphi University School of Social Work. She was an adjunct assistant professor at Hofstra University, teaching the course Separation and Loss. Gwen has delivered papers related to her bereavement work at national and international conferences.

At ninety-three, Gwen continues to inspire others by sharing her wisdom and life lessons at women's events. She and her husband, George, a retired lawyer and accountant, reside near Boston and cherish their vibrant community and family.

www.ingramcontent.com/pod-product-compliance
Lightning Source LLC
Chambersburg PA
CBHW030448100526
44580CB00002B/30